Water Management System in the Desert Region of Rajasthan

(Thirteenth-Eighteenth Centuries)

Water Management System in the Desert Region of Rajasthan

(Thirteenth-Eighteenth Centuries)

Jibraeil

Assistant Professor

Centre of Advanced Study

Department of History

Aligarh Muslim University

Ane Books Pvt. Ltd.

New Delhi ♦ Chennai ♦ Mumbai

Water Management System in the Desert Region of Rajasthan

(Thirteenth-Eighteenth Centuries)

Jibraeil

Published by

Ane Books Pvt. Ltd.

4821, Parwana Bhawan, 1st Floor, 24 Ansari Road, Darya Ganj,
New Delhi - 110 002, Tel.: +91(011) 23276843-44, Fax: +91(011) 23276863
e-mail: kapoor@anebooks.com, Website: www.anebooks.com

Branches

- Avantika Niwas, 1st Floor, 19 Doraiswamy Road, T. Nagar,
  Chennai - 600 017, Tel.: +91(044) 28141554, 28141209
  e-mail: anebookschennai@gmail.com, rathinam@anebooks.com
- Flat No. 03, Neel Suman C.H.S. Ltd., Mhasoba Maidan,
  Near Sampada Hospital, Kalyan West,
  Mumbai -421 301, Tel.: +919619192440, 9892381497
  e-mail: anebooksmum@mtnl.net.in, anebooksmum@gmail.com

ISBN : 978-93-8676-144-6

Printed at Replika Press Pvt. Ltd., New Delhi

To

Professor B.L.Bhadani

and

Mrs. Sarla Bhadani

Preface

It is a universally accepted truth that life originated from water. Water sustains life of humans, animals and plants; it is the most valuable and renewable natural resources on the earth. No doubt total quantity of water covers three-fourth of the globe, but not all drops are consumable. The geologists are of the opinion that there is enough fresh water available to fulfill all human needs. The irony is that it is not evenly distributed. Here arises the problem of conserving and preserving water–a problem that has perpetually boggled the human mind. Man has come a long way in devising unique and excellent methods to conserve and preserve water to fulfill his basic needs.

More than half of the world's population depends on ground water for its survival; the scenario in India is not much different. Ground water plays a vital role in meeting the water requirements of agriculture, industrial and domestic sectors in India. The importance of this precious natural resource can be gauged with the fact that more than 85 percent of India's rural domestic water requirements, more than 50 percent of its irrigation water requirements, and 50 percent of its urban water requirements are met from ground resources.

It is a fact that water is a scarce commodity in deserts. Today, even in the second decade of the twenty-first century more than 30 crore people are struggling to obtain drinking water in many regions of India. The people residing in the deserts of Rajasthan have been facing acute problems to procure water for daily chores, not to speak of the availability of potable water. Hence, utilization

of water for irrigation purposes sounds a far-fetched thing. But this has been made possible by the inhabitants of Rajasthan deserts. The harvesting of rain water, most of which goes waste, is an incredible solution to meet water shortage. In case water is not conserved, the water table would continue to recede further and further creating insurmountable adverse conditions in future. The following lines are really thought-provoking in the present scenario of water scarcity the world is threatened with:

Grandfather saw it in River
Father saw it in Well.
We saw it in Tap
Our children see it in Bottles.
Where will our grandchildren see it !!
In Capsule ???
If we still neglect,
It will be seen in Tears.

In Rajsthan we find *talabs* and *talais*, local turns used for water reservoirs situated in valleys and natural depressions. Some of the *talabs* have less deep wells in their beds called *beris*. Special care was has been taken to maintain the catchments (*agor*) of each *talab*. These *talabs* serve as the main source of water for the human and animal population in the deserts of Rajasthan even today. In this regard, the author of the book with a survey team, consulted many records and have also met experienced people and elder men at the survey sites (i.e., Phalodi, Nagaur, Bikaner, Churu and Jaisalmer), and have surprisingly come to know that during the medieval period too the people living in Rajasthan deserts ingenuously planned and created many water bodies including *talab, talais, kuwan, baowri, jhalara* and *nallah*. Mostly these water bodies were developed by various nobles, queens, kings, traders and others, and named after or by them. For example, Ghadsisar Talab in Jaisalmer, Ranisar Talab and Seth Sangidas Ka Kuwan in Phalodi, Lakeshwar Baowri

and Acharyon Ka Kuwan in Bikaner. Some of the *talabs* in the said areas have still maintained their identity. A few receive financial aid time to time from the state government for the repair work. But most of them are not in good condition because of unplanned modernization and urbanization. The catchments' area of the water bodies, particularly those of *talabs* have been captured by some of the influential locals or by the industrialists to set up new industries in the *agor* region of the *talabs*. Some of the water bodies are still alive and their water is still being used, though for animals and other purposes by the local population. More or less the catchment's areas of *talabs* have been destroyed and residential buldings have been constructed residential buildings there in its *agor*. Therefore, most of the existing water bodies of the surveyed areas have been either dried up or are in a very poor condition. The forts of the surveyed areas have good water harvesting system; hence the supply of water inside the monuments of the forts is quite adequate. Generally, inside fort complexes, wells were used to supply water to the various buildings. However, in few forts beautiful *baowris* were used for the purpose.

The present work on *Water Management System in the Desert Region of Rajasthan (Thirteenth-Eighteenth Centuries)* contains six chapters on one central theme concerning how the people of Rajasthan have been collecting small drops of water to use for drinking as well as irrigation purposes.The First Chapter is an Introduction. The Second and Third Chapters on the Marwar region discuss water harvesting and irrigation techniques adopted by the Paliwal Brahmins in Phalodi, as well as by the farmers in Nagaur to produce different crops including wheat, gram, barley, pulses and certain vegetables. In the Fourth and Fifth Chapters on the Bikaner state (i.e., Bikaner; Churu, Chhapar and Bidasar) explains about the rain water harvesting and the cultivation method either in small fields or in *bagichi* of the towns. Lastly the Sixth Chapter is on Jaisalmer, in which an attempt is made to elucidate

particularly about the *khadeen*, a technique which was adopted for the first time by the Paliwal Brahmins.Gradually it flourished when the farmers and cultivators of the region began to develop it. This method is still popular and in operation in many areas of Jaisalmer.

I must mention here that the idea to write this book came to me during my association with Prof. B.L. Bhadani. I was working with him as a Project Fellow in his project on INSA, New Delhi. No doubt he was the first to inspire me and provide me some relavant materials on the key plan of the water bodies to write this book on the present theme. I have also published jointly with him research papers in the *Proceedings of Rajasthan History Congress*, and in an edited national seminar proceedings entitled, *Urbanization and Trade Routes of Rajasthan*. These papers now have been modified and refined by the author, and incorporated as two chapters in this book. Prof. Ali Athar (Department of History, Aligarh Muslim University) also kept encouraging me during the progress of the book. I am grateful to both of them for their precious support. My friends Dr. Mayank Kumar, (Associate Professor, Satyawati College-Evening, University of Delhi), Dr. Tahsinur Rahman Warsi (Associate Professor, Department of Architecture, Aligarh Muslim University) and Dr. Shams Imran (Assistant Professor, Maulana Azad National Urdu University, Hyderabad) were keen to help me in getting this work published. Being an architect Dr. Warsi was involved in examining the ground plan of the water bodies. Prof. Inayat Ali Zaidi and Prof. Sunita Zaidi (Department of History and Culture, Jamia Millia Islamia University, New Delhi), Prof. Yaqub Ali Khan and Prof. M. Afzal Khan (Aligarh Muslim University), Prof. Jigar Mohammad (Department of History, University of Jammu & Kashmir), Prof. Ayub Ali Khan (Kakatiya University, Warangal), Dr. Suresh Mishra (M.P.), Dr. Manohar Singh Ranavat (Director, Natnagar Shodh Sansthan, Sitamau, M.P.), Dr. Firdos Anwar (Kirori Mal College, University of Delhi), Dr. Nasim Ahmad Khan (Aligarh), Prof. S. P. Vyas (JNV University,

Jodhpur) and Prof. V.K. Vashishtha (Jaipur) also encouraged me to complete this task. I extend my thanks to all of them for their guidance, suggestions and cooperation in publishing this work. The colleagues and staff of the Centre of Advanced Study, Department of History, Aligarh Muslim University, equally deserve special mention for their kind support and help.

Mr. Zameer Ahmad (Technical Assistant, Archaeology, Aligarh Muslim University) and Mr. Faiz Habib (Senior Cartographer, Department of History, Aligarh Muslim University) deserve special appreciation for preparing 'ground plan' of the water bodies and 'maps' of the towns, respectively. My thanks are also due to the staff of the Research Library, Department of History, Aligarh Muslim University, Aligarh; Rajasthan State Archives, Bikaner, Rajasthan and the locals and elders of the area who cooperated with us during the interviews willingly at the sites surveyed by us.

It is not possible for me to express due regards to my respected parents Janab Haji Hasan Raza Sahab and Mrs. Kitab-un-Nisha, my brothers, uncles, cousins and other close relations, whose love, fondness, and prayers have given me enormous help in all ups and downs of my life, and their full support and generosity has been a source of abiding inspiration throughout my life. At this moment, how can I forget the sacrifices made by my wife Mrs. Priyanka Singh F. Naaz and two sons Ahmad Zaid and Ahmad Saim. Their indulgence and firm support sustained me during my frequent and long visits to Rajasthan to collect data and survey the sites.

Finally, I am thankful to Mr. Sunil Saxena (Director), Mr. Jai Raj Kapoor (CEO), ANE BOOKS and Dr. Rita Mehra (Editor) for their diligent work in bringing out this book timely.

JIBRAEIL

Contents

Abbreviations

Ain	:	*Ain-i-Akbari*
ASL	:	Anoop Sanskrit Library, Bikaner
CSE	:	Centre for Science and Environment
EI	:	Epigraphia Indica
GOS	:	Gaekwad's Oriental Series, Baroda
INSA	:	Indian National Science Academy
JSP	:	Jaina Satya Prakasa, Ahmedabad
Khyat	:	Muhnot Nainsi, *Khyat*
NSS	:	Natnagar Shodh Sansthan, Sitamau
ONS	:	Ojha Nibandha Samgraha, Udaipur
PIHC	:	Proceedings of Indian History Congress
PR	:	Peterson's Report, Bombay, 1883 - 84
NWHN	:	National Water Harvesters Network
PRHC	:	Proceedings of Rajasthan History Congress
RB	:	Rajasthani Bharati, Bikaner
RSA	:	Rajasthan State Archives, Bikaner
RORI	:	Rajasthan Oriental Research Institute
Tod	:	Colonel James Tod, *Annals and Antiquities of Rajasthan*
Vir Vinod	:	Shyamal Das, *Vir Vinod*
VS	:	Vikram Samvat

List of Figures

1

Introduction

Agricultural technology in medieval India has come under scholarly focus in the last few decades. In this context, irrigational methods and devices form important components of agricultural practices. The study on the techniques and management of water harvesting for the purpose of field irrigation and the ensuing shifts and changes in the pattern of agriculture in the medieval times is still quite fascinating. Studies carried out by scholars of medieval India are of general nature. Professor Irfan Habib, in his monumental work, rightly emphasizes the importance of 'artificial irrigation' as an important aspect of Indian agriculture[1]. India is a vast country where peasants of different regions have employed numerous kinds of irrigational methods. However, it is high time to examine irrigational technology at regional levels. If one view characterizes India as a 'hydraulic civilization'[2], another holds 'that irrigation formed an important branch of administration in the past' and some remarkable "irrigation projects" were undertaken by the rulers of ancient and medieval India[3]. However, H.C.Verma[4] in one of his works argues that the country hardly had any "artificial irrigation"[5]

till the eighteenth century. It is only in the nineteenth century (1866) "a new policy" regarding the increase and improvement in the agricultural sector through 'artificial irrigation' was launched by Lord Lawrence that led to the opening of new big canals running into thousands of miles in northern India in general, and Punjab in particular, where "colony canals" formed "a class by themselves"[6]. But our study (literary, archaeological data and survey) proved that 'artificial irrigation' in dry region, particularly in 'Rajasthan Deserts' was created as a technique for irrigation specially by Paliwal Brahmins (discussed in details in Chapter 2 and Chapter 6) in the early and medieval period. So we are able to say that in 'Rajasthan Deserts' the 'artificial techniques' for irrigation already were in practice, i.e., *qilla nallah* (*bahlau* term used by Nainsi)[7], *khadeen* (explained in details by B.L. Bhadani[8] and Anil Agrawal and Sunita Narayan[9]), and *bandha*[10] in Jaisalmer (author himself surveyed the sites of Jaisalmer)

The study of these medieval irrigational water structures and 'artificial irrigation' can be carried out in two ways: first, by consulting contemporary records, and second by the physical surveys of the surviving bodies. The latter method appeared more feasible for surveying the water monuments because no records in a systematic manner were maintained in pre-modern times, specifically about their technological aspects. One may, therefore, quite legitimately suppose that this provided understanding of the irrigation technologies would be trustworthy, and it is supported by the archaeological evidence obtained through physical surveys.

The surveys and studies of medieval irrigational works in Rajasthan were initiated by scholars like B.D. Chattopadhyaya[11], Iqtidar Alam Khan and Ravindra Kumar[12]. Iqtidar Alam Khan's

'Structure, Location and Working of a Seventeenth Century Dyke at Kishangarh'[13], B.L. Bhadani's 'Indra Sarovar Dam: In Service of the Royal Family Deity and the People'[14], and 'Udai Sagar: A Sixteenth-Century Dam in Udaipur'[15], R. Thomas Rosin's 'Locality and Frontier: Securing Livelihood in the Aravalli Zone of Central Rajasthan'[16], and Anil Agrawal and Sunita Narayan's edited work. *Dying Wisdom, Rise, Fall and Potential of India's Traditional Water Harvesting Systems.*[17] Besides, a journalistic but useful survey of wells and tanks was conducted by Anupam Mishra[18]. His survey is primarily based on the oral evidence in the form of interviews. He compiled information on the techniques and methods of the construction of wells and tanks in the desert area. No comprehensive survey has been done on different regions of Rajasthan. Systematic physical survey of irrigational works of different localities is necessary to understand the level of efforts of peasants in different geographical and topographical settings.

With the above perspective we had decided to proceed to investigate various methods in different localities. For that first we had consulted and compiled contemporary documents for Marwar, Bikaner and Jaisalmer which could be a baseline for our physical survey of the irrigational works.

MARWAR

The evidence on Marwar is compiled by Muhnot Nainsi. His two works proved very beneficial for the purpose. His monumental work *Marwar-ra-Pargana-ri-Vigat*[19] is a villagewise gazetteer of Marwar which is a treasurehouse of information. It provides various means and modes of irrigational system for Marwar. He enumerated different kinds of wells: *chanch*, *kosita*, *dhimra* or *dhibra, kohar* and *kuwa.*

Besides describing different kinds of wells, Nainsi sometimes records the depth of water in terms of *hath* (*purus*/hands) in different localities which specifies the kind of well to be dug there. The interesting thing about Nainsi's information is that he puts the wells and water-lifting devices under one nomenclature. The *chanch* is a shallow well with the *dhenkli* mechanism. *Dhenkli*, based on the principle of lever, could only be used in shallow wells where water level is not more than six to nine feet below the surface. The *kosita* well most probably was operated by the *charas*. Presumably, *kosita* was not a shallow well, since two different apparatus, viz., *charas* and sometimes Persian-wheel were used to take outwater. Nainsi records the depth of water for *kosita* well with a Persian-wheel (45 feet to 84 feet, recorded in terms of *hath* and *purus*), and without a Persian-wheel from 15 to 45 feet. Thus, Nainsi's evidence indicates that where water was comparatively near the surface, *charas* was used; and where the water level was much lower, recourse was taken to Persian-wheel.[20] Thus, the information for the seven *parganas* of Marwar, namely Jodhpur, Merta, Jaitaran, Sojhat, Pokaran, Phalodi and Jalor is exhaustive and helps us in carrying out a physical survey of the structure. Nainsi's *Khyat* too offers data on water-harvesting bodies in different parts of Marwar. In addition to it, it gives important information on Mewar and Jaisalmer. For the Jalor *pargana* the evidence is compiled in two *Jalor Vigats* (two separate manuscripts)[21] preserved in the Natnagar Shodh Sansthan, Sitamau (M.P.).

Both *bahis* contain village-wise information on water bodies of Jalor. Similarly, the data for the adjoining *pargana* Sanchor was compiled by an anonymous person. This information is edited by N.S. Bhati and appended in the second volume of the *Vigat*.[22] Besides this consolidated treatise, scattered evidences about each *pargana* has been published at different places. Two important documents on water bodies are available in the

bahis of Marwar. One document offers data on various water-harvesting structures constructed at various places by the rulers, queens and the officials of the state.[23] Second document contains the number of water bodies inside and outside wall of the city of Jodhpur.[24] Besides these two, one list is available in the *Vigat* which gives a description of all kinds of buildings such as palaces, forts, temples, step-wells, wells and tanks built by the rulers during different periods. We have selected only water structures and appended them in the end[25]. Similar data on other *parganas* of Marwar such as Nagaur, Maroth and Didwana are available in sources in the manuscript form.

JAISALMER

The data on means of irrigation and other water bodies are compiled by Nainsi in his *Khyat*.[26] He provides exhaustive information on the region. Besides Jaisalmer, he gives details about the water bodies built by different individuals in the middle of the desert. His evidence belongs to Bikampur, Birsalpur, Pugal, Chohtan, Kotra and Derawar, etc. Besides him, Bankidas also offers very significant data on the region.[27] Nathmal's *Tawarikh Jaisalmer* is extremely important for the study of the region.[28]

BIKANER

For the Rathor state of Bikaner, Dayal Das provides some information. His two books *Khyat*[29] and *Khyat Desh Darpan*[30] are of much use. The latter offers village-wise evidence. Both help us in locating the water-harvesting structures in different parts of the state.

Besides this, large numbers of *bahis* such as *kagad bahi, kamthana bahi, sava bahi,* etc. are available in the Rajasthan State Archives, Bikaner, which give village-wise information about water structures.

Inscriptions

Inscriptions are a very important source of information[31]. During the field survey, we have come across a large number of Rajasthani, Sanskrit and Persian inscriptions on the water bodies which provide details about the structures. These stone documents cover almost all the regions of our research areas. Many of them are published in the book form and numerous are available in the research journals.

The Jain Munis composed city-centred ghazals which contain information on the water-harvesting structures. Major cities of the states of Jodhpur, Bikaner, Jaisalmer Maroth, Sadri, Udaipur and Nagaur are covered by these saints. Some of these are published while large numbers are still in the form of manuscripts preserved in the branches of the Rajasthan Oriental Research Institute, and the Jain *bhandaras*. We have used these poetic treatises for the field work. Some of them are *Bikaner-Ki-Ghazal, Nagor-Ki-Ghazal,* [32] and *Jodhpur-Ki-Ghazal.* Besides this, an exclusive poetic composition on the tank of Gadsisar in Jaisalmer is available which gives the history of this remarkable structure of the desert.[33]

The principal objective of our studies has been to explore the technical aspects of the making of wells, dams, tanks and canals. Besides, types of wells and other means of irrigation at the village level have also been examined by us, based entirely on contemporary records. Going beyond textual evidence, the physical surveys of irrigational works are important for the understanding of the settlement pattern, levels of technology and the degree of peasants' awareness of ecology and environment.

The present work proposes to survey the structure of different kinds of wells (namely, *kuwa, kohar, beri, kosita* and

dhandh), *baowri* or *baori or baowadi* (step-wells), tanks, dams and canals. The term *baori* or *baowri* has two components–*ba* meaning water and *ori* or *wadi*, meaning enclosed corridor or steps. Basically it is a combination of two characteristics of two water structures: one is well, and the second is a chamber with descending steps reaching upto the mouth of well. The former was used for tapping underground water, while the latter for collecting rain water. So a well with an overhead structure attached with steps was styled as a step-well. It becomes clear from this that the *baori* was a peculiar type of well monument which was multipurpose, such as religious rituals, drinking and irrigation. However, the term *baoli* (Persian) does not appear in the Rajasthani documents[34]. In Delhi and Agra region step-well is known as *baoli* and in Rajasthan it is termed as *baori* or *bawari*[35]. In Gujarat, *vapi, vauvavdi, vai* are the terms used for the step-wells[36]. It is interesting to note that in the Indian classic *Shilpa Shashtra* and in its inscriptions, the word *vapi* and *vapika* have been used for step-wells[37]. In Rajasthan, step-well is referred to as *bauri* and *baori* in many accounts of travellers[38]. B. L. Bhadani in his book explains the step -wells of Rajasthan in detail. According to one of his explanations a step-well consists of four major components: 1) a vertical well; 2) an enclosed chamber, sometimes multistoried; 3) a flight of steps from the top pavilion coming down to the water level; and 4) intermediate platforms down to the water level[39]. He further discusses various types of step-wells located at different places. Broadly, these can be classified into atleast five categories according to their locations, such as (i) those connected to a temple or shrine (ii) those located in a portion of a garden or orchard complex (iii) those within or at the edge of a village (iv) those on highways and trade routes, and (v) those in the middle of an agricultural field or on the fringes of an inhabited area or field[40].

Khadeen cultivation was peculiar to Jaisalmer and the surrounding areas about which Nainsi offers precious information. It was an ingenious technique developed by local peasants. The motive behind these constructions was to drain water from the above *khadeens*, located on a higher ground, to adjoining areas. These are the finest examples of dam-use and canal technology made in pre-colonial period in the 'Thar Desert'. The magnitude of investments in waterworks and names/castes of the planners need much more investigation. It is hoped that further physical surveys of these structures by the researchers would bring out many more unknown aspects of irrigation system used in arid zones into light.

Our exploration and documentation of the surviving irrigational structures in Rajasthan desert enabled us to study certain important aspects of agricultural technology and economy of medieval Rajasthan. These are (1) techniques of utilization of groundwater; (2) means of rain-water harvesting; (3) the level of hydraulic knowledge of the rural population; (4) the quantum of area irrigated by these methods; (5) the level of expenditure on the device and economic return from it and its comparison with modern systems of irrigation; and (6) relationship of irrigation system with contemporary social organization.

Information concerning agricultural and irrigational systems are given in the *Vigat*, *Khyat*, archival and non-archival sources collected and incorporated in the chapters. In addition to it, a large number of folk songs, folk stories (*bat* literature) and proverbs related to water are found in different parts of Rajasthan, few of them are incorporated in some of the chapters of this book as well. These are extremely useful to understand the level of consciousness among the rural folks about water-harvesting. Specifically, the folk stories prove useful in providing an insight into water management system in the pre-modern times.

Recently, there has been an increased realization about the importance of ancient legends. European scholars believe that an analysis of ancient legends can transform our knowledge of earthquakes, volcanoes, and tsunamis. Therefore, the French scholars are involved in compiling tales or ancient legends. Similarly, the folk literature would provide a preliminary idea of areas to be chosen for field investigation. Archaeological explorations of the area are carried out. A detailed documentation of the structures was prepared in the form of line-drawings, ground-plans, photographs and maps. Besides the information on the structures, notes were also prepared on the surrounding agricultural land that have benefited from these facilities. Moreover, relevant revenue records as well as oral information collected from the sites are incorporated here with a view to understand in what way the irrigated areas differed from the non-irrigated areas.

It is expected that the present work will help in understanding the pattern of agricultural life, structure of agrarian society and the rural settlements in Rajasthan's desert region better. The physical surveys also resulted in the accumulation of different types of data, specifically folk songs and folk stories which would prove to be useful to other scholars working on the theme.

Geography

Col. James Tod appears to have been pioneer in choosing the term 'Rajasthan' as the title of his celebrated book[41]. But at the administrative level, the term has been derived from Rajputana. This nomenclature was given by the British to all the Rajput principalities[42]. In medieval times the terms Rajasthan or "Raythan" were employed to indicate the headquarters of the royal seat[43] of the Rajput rulers. Therefore, the term assumes

historical as well as cultural significance. Rajasthan, situated in the north-western part of India between 23°3′ N and 30°12′ N latitudes and 69°30′ E and 78°17′ E longitudes covers an areas of about 342,274 sq. km[44]. It is bounded on the east by Uttar Pradesh, on the south by Gujarat, on the west by Pakistan and in the north by Punjab and in the north-east by Haryana[45] [see Figure 1.1 Outline Map of Rajasthan].

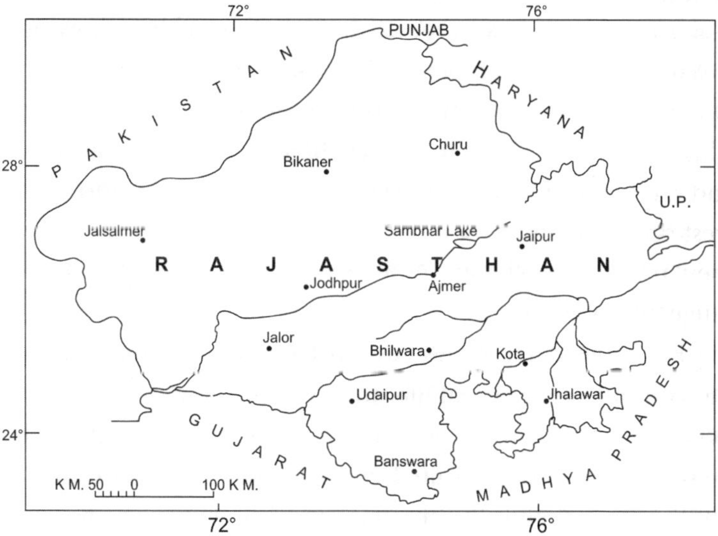

Figure 1.1 Outline map of Rajasthan

Geographically, Rajasthan is divided into plains and hilly regions. Plains lie between 24°30′ and 30°12′ N and 69°15′ and 76°45′ E, including the *Marushthali* (eastern portion of the Thar) and the adjoining Bagar (steppe land, to the west of the Aravallis) extending over the western districts of Rajasthan, namely Jaisalmer, Barmer, Jodhpur, Bikaner, Jalor, Nagaur, Ganganagar and Churu, along with the western portions comprising Pali, Sikar and Jhunjhunu districts. It covers an area of 196,747 sq. km.[46] The Aravali ranges[47] form the chief topographical feature

in Rajasthan, extending from Champaner in Gujarat in the north-easterly direction upto near Delhi, covering 692 km[48]. It divides the province into two natural divisions, viz, the north-west and south-east of the Aravali; about three-fifth of Rajasthan lies north-west of this line, and comprises mainly desert and semi-desert regions. Its extent is about 60,000 sq. miles and covers the former states of Jaisalmer, Bikaner, major portions of Jodhpur and a part of Jaipur.[49] It is dry, lacks-water and is less productive, as far as agriculture is concerned. The south-eastern region is formed of the modern districts of Banswara, Dungarpur, Udaipur, Bhilwara, Bundi, Kota and Jhalawar[50]. This region is more hilly, and comparatively gets more water, and consequently more wooded and rich in agriculture[51]. The western and southern part of the Aravali is drained by rivers and their tributaries. The major river the Luni rises in the Aravali range and flows in the south-west direction. It is finally lost in the Rann of Kutch. It has several tributaries mostly rising in the Aravali hills, neither the main nor any of its tributaries is perennial. Nainsi describes at length the area through which various rivers run and also mentions the streams that join the Luni[52]. The junction of the two rivers, the Gilari (Guhiya) and Sukri, at Sojhat support a small fertile tract[53].

The western part of Rajasthan, particularly Jaisalmer, Bikaner and Barmer is marked by sand-dunes. This part is well punctuated by exposed rock surface[54]. The rainfall is 10 cm per year and the use of transport is difficult. The features of physiography, the climate and aridity have made this area inhospitable[55]. The soils of Rajasthan plain are generally characterized as sandy containing 90 to 95 per cent sand and 5 to 7 per cent clay[56]; red desert soil covers Nagaur, Jodhpur, Pali, Jalor, parts of Churu and Jhunjhunu districts[57]. Yellowish brown sandy soils extend over Nagaur and Pali districts[58]. Other

types of soil, i.e., red sandy, clay loam, red sandy loam and loam (alluvial types) soils are limited in their extent and less important for the location of settlement[59]. However, the loam (alluvial type) is significant for cultivation as well as for large and prosperous rural settlements in the areas of Neem-ka-Thana and Khetri[60]. In the sandy region cover is very thin and only a few small trees can be observed here and there. Large areas are covered with scrubby which are thorny and have a stunted growth[61]. The western arid and semi-arid part of the state is an important area in livestock production. This industry provides subsidiary occupations to the desert inhabitants, particularly the nomadic tribes who depend for their livelihood on their livestock[62].

The major areas selected for this book form the major portion of the 'Thar Desert' in Rajasthan.

Bikaner, erstwhile headquarters of a royal seat, derives its name from Rao Bika, founder of the dynasty. 'Ner' literally means a 'settlement' or a habitation. Tradition also says that Naira was the name of the owner of the site who parted with it on the condition that his name should be linked with Rao Bika, and hence the name Bikaner.[63] It lies in the north-western part of Rajasthan, and is located between 27°54′ and 74°12′ east longitude[64]. It is suronded by several districts, like in the north leis Ganganagar, in the west Jaisalmer and Bahawalpur (West Pakistan), in the east Churu and Ganganagar and in south-east and south Nagaur and Jodhpur[65]. With an average rainfall ranging from 12.70 cm. to 25.40 cm. (5″ to 10″), there is practically no surface runoff. Therefore, it can boast of no river worth-mentioning the name. Bikaner has always been the most important trading, manufacturing and cultural centre for the state of Rajasthan. Being the capital city of Rajasthan state, it has got political importance and has emerged as a centre of excellence in the field of art and culture[66].

Jodhpur derives its name from its Rathor chief, Rao Jodha in AD 1459[67]. It was a *pargana* and *sarkar* headquarters during the time of Akbar. Rao Jodha and subsequent rulers made this city as their seat of government. The Rathor principality was also known as Marwar which extended to a very large area. In modern times it was divided in many districts and all of them come under our study. The district stretches roughly from 26°0′ and 27°37′ north latitude to 72°55′ and 73°52′ east longitude[68]. The maximum length of the district from north to south is 197 km, and it borders five other districts of Rajasthan. Jodhpur is bounded on the north by Bikaner and Jaisalmer; on the south by Barmer and Pali; on the east by Pali and Nagaur; and on the west by Jaisalmer[69]. The district resembles an irregular rectangle in shape, whose longer sides are slightly squeezed. The northern-most part of the northern segment of the district comprises the Phalodi tehsil, the centrally situated tehsil of Shergarh.Osian conjointly form a rectangle and are equally divided by a common border, with Shergarh occupying the western half, having a common border with Phalodi in the north, Osian in the east and Jodhpur in the south-east. Osian occupies the eastern half of the rectangle forming common border with Phalodi on the north, Shergarh on the west, Jodhpur in the south and Bilara on the east[70]. The average height of the district above the mean sea level is between 250 and 300 mts. The general slope is towards the west[71]. In this arid region sand-dunes present a common sight[72]. The Luni, which rises near Pushkar in Ajmer, is the only river of any importance flowing through Jodhpur. After flowing through the portions of Nagaur and Pali, it enters Jhak village in the Bilara tehsil of Jodhpur. Its water is stored to form a huge artificial lake known as Jaswantsagar.[73] The total length of the river in the district is about 122 km and it flows for most of the period during the year. Mitri is its chief tributary, which enters the district near the village of Khoaspura in the Bilara[74].

Jaisalmer, the western-most region of the Rajasthan desert, is completely blanketed by sand-dunes. It extends from south to north along the border of India and Pakistan[75]. Jaisalmer was founded by King Jaisa[76] or Jaisal. The word Jaisalmer is derived from a combination of two words: Jaisal and Meru-Jaisal's fort[77]. The district is situated in the extreme west of Rajasthan and forms the major part of the Great Indian Desert. It is located between 26°01′ to 28°02′ north latitude and 69°29′ to 72°20′ east longitude[78]. Jaisalmer is bounded on the west, north and north-west by Pakistan and on the north-east by Bikaner. On its south lies the district of Barmer and on the east the district of Jodhpur[79]. It is sandy, dry and ill-watered, unkind to all forms of life, animals and plants[80]. The entire areas is barren and dreary, the only variations on the landscape being a few hills and many sand-dunes[81]. The land covered by the district slopes towards the Indus Valley and the Rann of Kutch[82].

There is not a single perennial river in the district. A few streams flow around Jaisalmer town, during the rainy season. The streams are shallow and water seeps through the porous sand very quickly. The stream inundates the area near Dheda village and forms a shallow stretch of water known as *masoori khadeen*.When the water dries up, wheat and gram are grown in the area. Most of the seasonal streams are only *nullahs* with limited catchment areas. The waters are locked by the inhabitants to form *khadeen* used for cultivation[83]. There are many water bodies but no natural lakes in the district. During the rainy season water accumulates in several low-lying areas called *khadeens.* After the water dries up *jowar*, wheat and gram are grown on the beds [84]. Therefore, we are able to say that there has been an endless struggle in Jaisalmer for survival which is reflected in all aspects of life of its inhabitants.

NOTES

1. Irfan Habib, *Agrarian System of Mughal India*, second revised edition, Oxford University Press, Delhi, 1999, pp.1-67. [Irfan Habib also writes that in the sixteenth and seventeenth centuries, the arid regions of Punjab were turned into rich agricultural areas because of the construction of a large number of wells. For more details see Irfan Habib, 'Technology Changes and Society-13th and 14th Centuries' (Presidential Address), Varanasi, *PIHC*, 1969, pp. 153-154. Also see Chetan Singh, *Punjab in the Seventeenth Century*, Oxford University Press, Delhi, 1988, pp. 93-98.
2. Karl Wittfogel, *Oriental Despotism: A Comparative Study of Total Power, Passim* (As quoted by H.C.Verma, *Harvesting Water and Rationalization of Agriculture in North Medieval India (Thirteenth-Sixteenth Centuries),* Anamika Publishers, Delhi, 2001.
3. R.C. Majumdar, H.C.Ray Chaudhuri and Kalikinkar Datta, *An Advanced History of India*, Fourth Edition, 1990, p.864.
4. H.C.Verma, *Harvesting Water and Rationalization of Agriculture in North Medieval India (Thirteenth-Sixteenth Centuries),* op. cit., p.1.
5. R.C. Majumdar, H.C.Ray Chaudhuri and Kalikinkar Datta, op. cit., p.564.
6. Ibid., p. 864.For a detailed study one may be referred to Elizabeth Whitecombe, 'Canal Irrigation and Ecological Change in Colonial North India', in *Social Ecology*, ed., Ramchandra Guha, Oxford University Press, Delhi, 1994, pp.132-149.
7. B.L. Bhadani and Jibraeil, 'Techniques of Irrigation in the Desert Area of Phalodi in Medieval Times', Proceedings of the *Rajasthan History Congress*, Bikaner, 2008, pp.36-43.
8. B.L.Bhadani,'Jaisalmer Settlement Pattern, Dam Technology and Economy in the First Half of the Seventeenth Century', Felicitation Volume of Professor Agam Kumar Mathur, Dadaji Maharaj Abhinandan Granth, Vol. III, Hajuri Bhavan, Agra,

July 27, 1995, pp. 149-157. *Khadeen* in and around Kuldhara Settlement described by S.Ali Nadeem Rezavi in his well-researched survey based paper entitled, 'Kuldhara in Jaisalmer State-Social and Economic Implications of the Remains of a Medieval Settlement', in Proceedings of the *Indian History Congress*, 56th Session, Rabindra Bharti, Calcutta, 1995, pp.312-38.

9. Anil Agrawal and Sunita Narayan, eds., *Dying Wisdom, Rise, Fall and Potential of India's Traditional Water Harvesting System*,' reprint, CSE, Delhi, 2005.Also explained by S. Ali Nadeem Rezavi, 'Kuldhara in Jaisalmer State –Social and Economic Implications of the Remains of a Medieval Settlement',op. cit., pp. 312-38 and Mayank Kumar, 'Adaption to Climatic Variability: Irrigation and Settlement Patterns in Early Medieval Rajasthan', in *Medieval History Journal*, Sage Publication, Delhi, 2014, pp.57-86.
10. *Bandhs* are made at levels higher than the fields to be irrigated. These *bandhs* thus prevent the mansoon rain draining away rapidly and are able to supply water to the crops in the lands below by slow percolation. For such techniques see B.Ray, *Census 1961: West Bengal District Census Handbook*, Bankura, 1967, p. 138. Also see Chapter 6 of this book.
11. B.D.Chattopadhyaya, 'Irrigation in Early Medieval Rajasthan', *Journal of the Economic and Social History of the Orient*, 1973, pp. 298-316.
12. Iqtidar Alam Khan and Ravindra Kumar, 'The Mansagar Dam of Amber' *Technology in Ancient and Medieval India*, eds., Aniruddha Ray and S.K. Bagchi, Sundeep Publication, Delhi, 1986, pp. 25-40.
13. Iqtidar Alam Khan, 'Structure, Location and Working of a Seventeenth Century' paper presented to the *Indian History Congress*, 1984 (cyclostyled).
14. B.L. Bhadani, 'Indra Sarovar Dam: In Service of the Royal Family Deity and the People', Felicitation Volume of Professor Anand Krishna, *The Anandvana of Indian Art*, 2004.

15. B.L. Bhadani, 'Udai Sagar: A Sixteenth Century Dam in Udaipur', *Medieval India-2*, ed., Shahabuddin Iraqi, Manohar, Delhi, 2008, pp.273-88.
16. R.Thomas Rosin, 'Locality and Frontier: Securing Livelihood in the Aravalli zone of Central Rajasthan', *The Idea of Rajasthan*, II, eds., Karine Sahomer, Joan L. Eradman, Desyck O. Lodrick and Lylord I. Rudolf, Delhi, 2001.
17. *Dying Wisdom, Rise, Fall and Potential of India's Traditional Water Harvesting System*,'op. cit.
18. Anupama Mishra, *Rajasthan Ki Rajat Bundeyen*, Gandhi Shanti Pratisthan, Delhi, 1995 and *Aaj Bhi Khare Hain Talab*, second edition, Gandhi Shanti Pratisthan, Delhi, 1994.
19. Munhata Nainsi, *Marwar-ra-pargana-ri-Vigat*, ed., N.S. Bhati, Vol. I (1968), II (1969), and III (1974), Rajasthan Oriental Research Institute, Jodhpur.
20. B.L. Bhadani, *Peasants, Artisans and Entrepreneurs, Economy of Marwar in the Seventeenth Century*, Rawat Publication, Jaipur, 1999, pp.41-42.
21. *Jalor Vigats* (big and small *bahi*), MSS, Natnagar Shodh Sansthan, Sitamau, Madhya Pradesh.
22. *Vigat*, II, pp.373-408
23. *Vigat*, II, pp.579-95.
24. Ibid., pp.596-602.
25. Ibid., pp.559-78.
26. Nainsi, *Khyat*, ed., B.P. Sakariya, II, Jodhpur, 1962.
27. *Bankidas-ri-Khyat*, ed., Narottam Das Swami, Jaipur, 1956.
28. Nathmal, *Jaisalmer Tawarikh*, Jaisalmer.
29. *Dayal Das-ri-Khyat*, ed., Dashrath Sharma and Dina Nath Khatri, Bikaner.
30. Dayal Das, *Khyat Des Darpan*, ed., Girija Shankar Sharma, Bikaner, 1980.
31. *Rajasthan Ke Abhilekh*, ed., Govind Lal Srimali, 2 Vols, Maharaja Mansingh Pushtak Prakashan, Jodhpur, 2000.

32. *Nagarvarnatmak Hindi Padya Sangrah*, ed., Muni Kanti Sagar, Surat, 1948.
33. Anupam Mishra, *Aaj Bhi Khare-Hein Talab*, op. cit., pp.102-5.
34. B.L.Bhadani, *Water Harvesting, Conservation and Irrigation in Mewar (AD 800-1700),* Manohar, Delhi, 2012, pp.171-172 (and Chapter 8 on Step-Wells.).
35. Jutta Jain Neubauer, *The Step Wells of Gujarat in Art Historical Perspective,* Abhinav Publication, New Delhi, 1981, p.XIII; M. K. Pundhir, 'Banjaron Ki Baori at Sikar (Rajasthan): A Study of Medieval Hydrauloc Technology' in *Medieval India 3 Researches in the History of India*, ed., B.L. Bhadani, Manohar, Delhi, 2012, p.235.
36. Ibid., p.1.
37. Ibid.
38. Col. James Tod, *Travels in Western India*, Orient Publishers, Delhi, 1971.
39. B.L.Bhadani, *Water Harvesting, Conservation and Irrigation in Mewar (AD 800-1700)*, op. cit., p. 172.
40. Ibid.
41. Col. James Tod, *Annals and Antiquities of Rajasthan*, Vols. I, II, and III, Humphrey Milford, Oxford University Press, London, 1920.
42. Ibid., Vol. I, p.1
43. Muhnot Nainsi, *Khyat*, ed., Badri Prasad Sakariya, Vol.I, Jodhpur, 1960.
44. V.C. Mishra, *Geography of Rajasthan,* National Book Trust, New Delhi, 1967, p. 1, Also *Census of India*, Vol. I, Part II-A, p. 84.
45. K.C. Jain, *Ancient Cities and Towns of Rajasthan,* Motilal Banarasidas, Delhi, 1972, pp. 19-20.
46. R.L. Singh, *India: A Regional Geography, National Geographical Society of India*, reprint, Varanasi, 1987, pp. 49-50.
47. According to the Geologists, it is the oldest mountain Chain of India. K.C. Jain, op.cit, pp. 19-20.

48. K.C. Jain, op. cit., pp. 19-20. Cf. V.C. Mishra, op. cit., p. 4.
49. Ibid., pp. 19-20.
50. Ibid.
51. Ibid.
52. B.L. Bhadani, *Peasants, Artisans and Entrepreneurs Economy of Marwar in the 17th Century,* op. cit., p. 5. Cf. Muhnot Nainsi, *Marwar-ra-pargana-ri-Vigat,* ed., Narain Singh Bhati, Vol.II, 1969, pp. 281-82.
53. Ibid.
54. Ibid., p. 1
55. Ibid., p. 3
56. R.L. Singh, op. cit., p. 57.
57. Ibid.
58. Ibid.
59. R.C. Sharma, *Settlement Geography of the Indian Desert*, Kumar Brothers, New Delhi, 1972. p. 29.
60. Ibid.
61. R.L. Singh, op. cit. p. 57.
62. Ibid.
63. *Rajasthan District Gazetteers,* Bikaner, ed., K.K. Sehgal, Government of Rajasthan, Jaipur, 1972, p.1.
64. Ibid.
65. Ibid.
66. R.C. Sharma, *Settlement Geography of the Indian Desert*, op. cit., pp. 138-139.
67. *Rajasthan District Gazetteers*, Jodhpur, ed., B.D. Agrawal, Government of Rajasthan, Jaipur, 1979, p.1.
68. Ibid.
69. Ibid.
70. Ibid.
71. Ibid.

72. Ibid., p.4
73. Ibid., pp.4-5
74. Ibid., p.5
75. R.C. Sharma, op. cit., p. 9.
76. G.N. Sharma, *Social Life in Medieval Rajasthan*, (1500-1800), L.N. Agarwal, Agra, 1968, p. 49
77. *Rajasthan District Gazetteers*, Jaisalmer, ed., K.K. Sehgal, Government of Rajasthan, Jaipur,1973, p. 1
78. Ibid.
79. Ibid.
80. Ibid., p.4
81. Ibid.
82. Ibid.
83. Ibid., p.6
84. Ibid.

■■■

2

Water Harvesting and Irrigation Techniques in Phalodi

It is fascinating to note that the area of Phalodi in Marwar region was an excellent example of extraordinary water management system. But gradually some of the water bodies got destroyed because of unplanned process of modernization and urbanization. People of this area must have seriously considered its water potential and strategic situations. In this regard we explored a large number of the surface as well as ground-water bodies in the urban and rural areas of *pargana* Phalodi in Marwar (see Appendix-2.1 and 2.2).

Phalodi, formerly was the headquarter of a district of the same name in Jodhpur state and now it is the headquarters of a *panchayat samiti* , *tehsil* and sub-division.[1] The town is situated about 70 miles in the north-west of Jodhpur city between 27°8′ N. and 72°22′ E.[2] It is said to have been founded around the middle of the fifteenth century.[3] In the *qasba* a fort was erected which is attributed to Hamir Singh , a grandson of Rao Suja. The fort has a capacious reservoir for water and some fine palaces too.[4] Some

16 kms to the north of the town a large depression called the Phalodi salt source or the *Rinn* is found.[5] This town at one time was granted to the chief of Jaisalmer by Mughal emperor Akbar and was subsequently included for a short time in Bikaner,[6] before it came into the hands of the Marwar Raj.[7] It has a good water supply and is well drained with very healthy water.[8] Even many of the *banias* of this town were very enterprising and traded beyond the borders of India, bringing back much wealth to the town.[9] The information related to water reservoir such as, *nallah* (channel or *bahlau*), ponds, *beras*[10] *beris*[11], *talabs* (tanks) and *kohars* (wells) are obtainable in Nainsi's *Vigat*.[12] Besides this, the information about the villages of *pargana* Phalodi are also mentioned in *Vigat*. They are known as Mokheri, Kheechan, Sabrig, Jaliwaro, Dahiya Kohar, Hupali, Chhila, Godhanli, Varnari, Naberi, and Meha Kohar.[13] From the above evidence it emerges that the water-harvesting management of all these units were outstanding. It is generally believed that the knowledge of the Paliwal Brahmans about the water management was excellent.

An attempt has been made in this chapter to verify the information given by Nainsi in the *Vigat*, especially about irrigational devices and water management of urban and rural areas of *pargana* Phalodi. We surveyed *qasba* Phalodi and its three adjacent villages, such as Mokheri, Khichan and Mohra.[14] The main aim of our survey was to find out more details about irrigational technique in medieval Marwar. The detailed work of our survey undertaken consists of two parts: first part deals with the field work on urban areas, while the second part covers the rural areas.

According to an old man and a temple purohit, this *qasba* was founded in VS 1515/AD 1458 in the name of *Phaladhi*, the daughter of Siddhuji Kala. This *qasba* has its own history and before its foundation, it was known as Vijayapatan which can be verified by Kalyan temple.[15] K.C. Jain[16] writes that Phalodi's early names were Vijayapura, and Vijayanagari. In the beginning, it was ruled by the Pavaras. An inscription of VS 1145/ AD 1088 in the temple of Kalyanaraya refers to Raja Hathadeva Pavara. The Lokesvara temple now known as the Kalyanaraya of Phalodhi, was famous in the twelfth century. The said inscription refers to Hathadeva Pavara probably in connection with some grant. This inscription proves that this temple existed earlier than the eleventh century. Another inscription of VS 1236/ AD 1179 records some privileges granted to it by Rana Katia, a feudatory of Prithviraja Chauhan of Ajmer. Though he lived at Bikampur, the headquarters of the Chauhan kingdom, but came to worship the deity of this place[17].

It is exactly not known, when the old name of Vijayapura got changed into that of Phalodhi. There was a period of obscurity in the life of this town. It seems that it might have been destroyed by the incessant incursions of Mohammedans, as also severe famines, which might have depopulated it. When the Pavaras lost their domain of Barmer, it became totally ruined. It was on the ruins of Vijayanagari that the new city of Phalodhi was founded around the middle of the fifteenth century by Rav Naro, the Rathor prince of Marwar[18]. Phalodhi, as also proved by inscriptions, is a derivation of Phalavardhika. This place is said to be named *Phuludhirovasa* from Phuludhi, after the name of a Pallivala Brahmani, who came to live there. Hence, Naro came to be called Phalodi[19].

A person Gopikisanji of Phalodi had compiled the history of the *qasba* but because of his untimely demise in the month of January 2008, the book could not see the light of the day. Experienced persons informed us which we also verified by our survey that this *qasba* is located in the depression. A contour map is prepared by me (author) with the help of Mr. Faiz Habib (Cartographer, Department of History, Aligarh Muslim University, Aligarh) to show the margin of the depression between villages and the *qasba* Phalod (see Figure 2.3 and 2.4). A *nallah* (locals called it *nadi* or *qila nadi*) passes through the west of the *qasba* and interestingly according to the information collected by us, most of the tanks, *taals* and *talais* are located on the right and left of this *nallah*[20]. Even numerous *beris* (small 40-60 feet deep wells) have been dug in the slope area which is presently known as *maliyon ka baas* (see Figure 2.1) In this locality peasants cultivated vegetables and both the crops i.e. *kharif* and *rabi* (see Figure 2.2 & 2.3).

Figure 2.1 Area of *maliyon ka baas*, *qasba* Phalodi

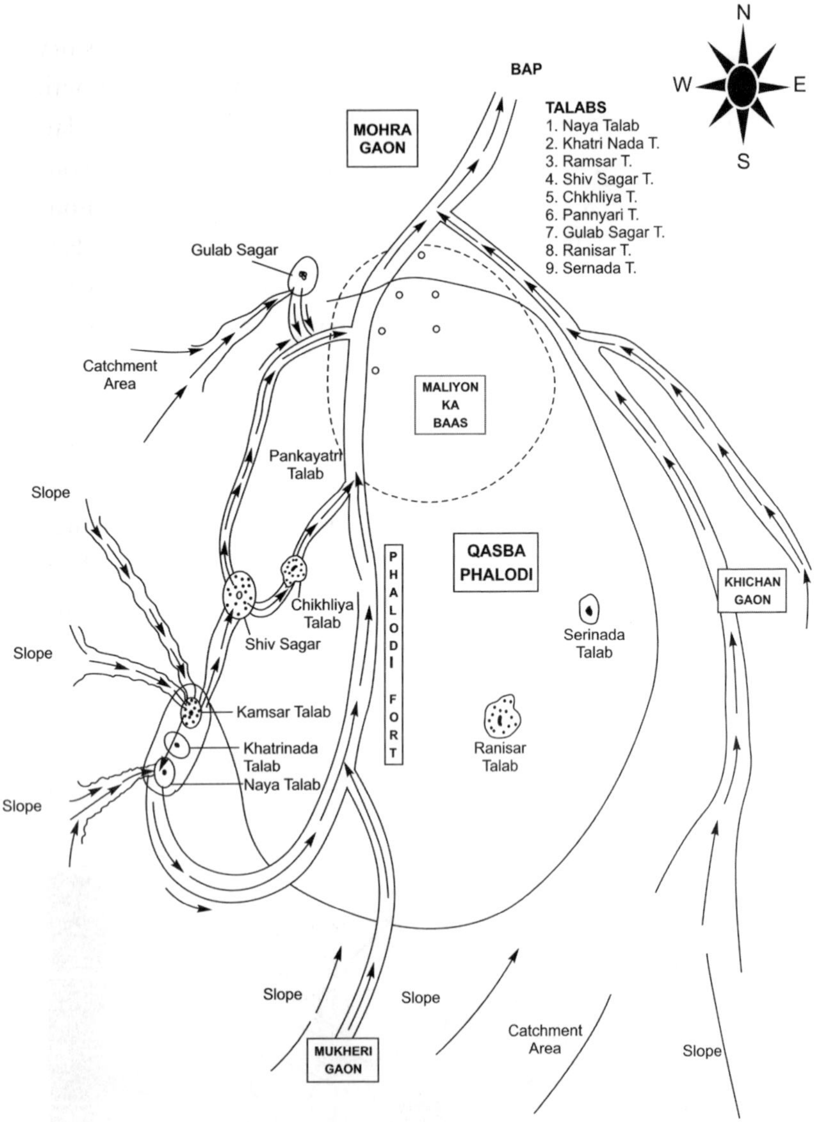

Figure 2.2 Ground plan of technique of water-harvesting and irrigation in medieval Phalodi, Rajasthan (not on scale)

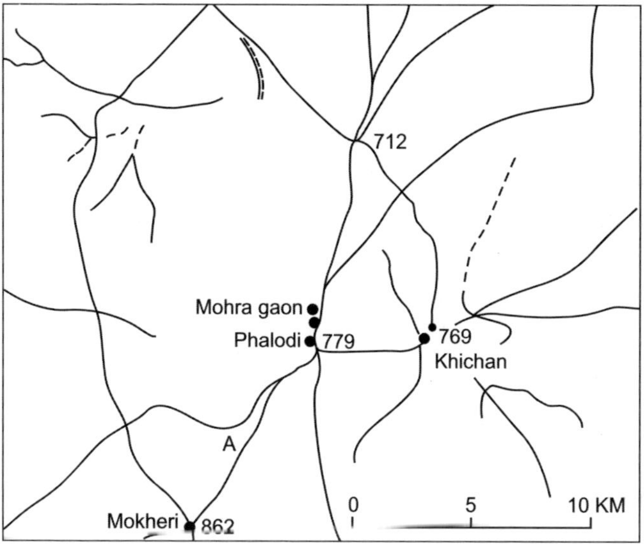

Figure 2.3 Phalodi on contour map

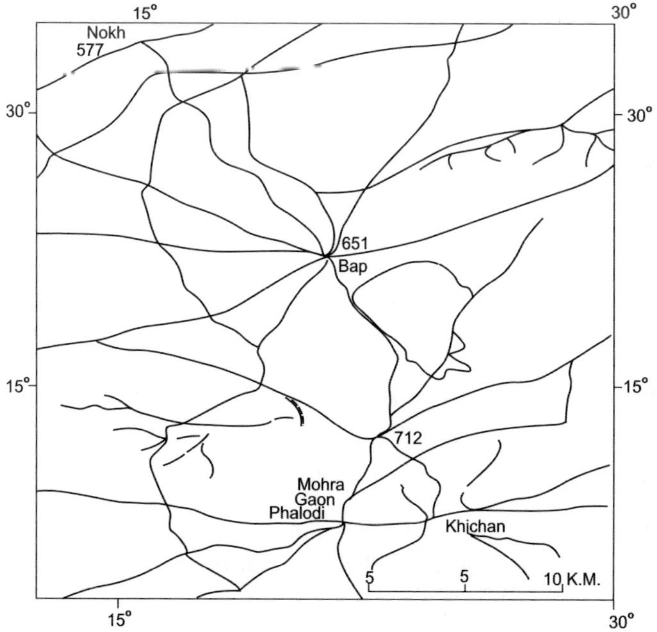

Figure 2.4 Slopes of villages towards *qasba* shown on contour map

In our survey we found many tanks are located in a row, such as Naya Talab, Khatrinada Talab, Ramsar Talab, Chikhliya Talab, Panihari Talai and Gulab Sagar. All these water bodies are located from south-west (west side from the *qasba)* to north (from the *qasba)*[21]. The water of these bodies goes to Mohra Gaon (situated 4 kms north of the *qasba*) and thus covers many more villages (see Figure 2.4). We have also got a beautiful sweet-water well and a few other salty wells, *beris* (small wells mostly constructed without tanks), *bera* (average deep well constructed with one or two tanks) and *kohar* (big well more than 350 feet deep constructed with four tanks). *Kohar's* water was used mainly for drinking purposes, while water of *beri* and *bera* was used for drinking as well as irrigation purposes. Details are mentioned below:

I

URBAN WATER BODIES OF PHALODI

WELLS

Seth Sangidas Ka Kuwa

Initially this well was dug by Rathors at the time of famine but it could not supply sweet water for drinking purposes. Later on a Brahman Seth Sangidas re-excavated at the depth of 360 feet (60 *Purus* = 60 × 6′) to get sweet water. This is a beautiful well having four octagonal tanks. It was used by different castes such as Brahman, Kshatriya, Vaishya and the menials. It is a four-sides operated well[22] (see Figure 2.5 and 2.6).

Four Tanks

North tank	-	Brahmans
South tank	-	Rajputs
West tank	-	general use
East tank	-	others

Presently this well is not in use (see Figure 2.5 & 2.6 of Sangidas well)

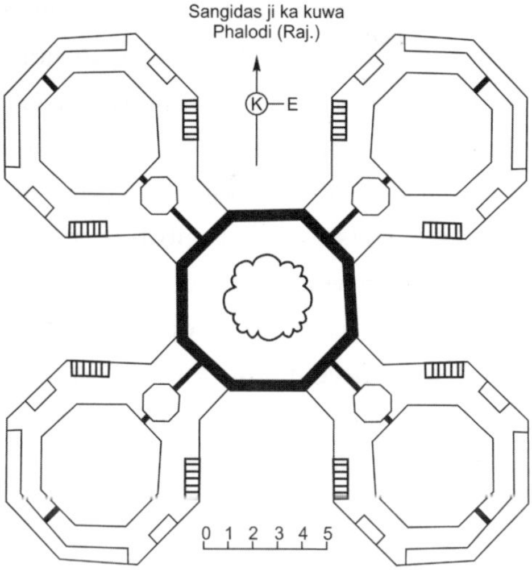

Figure 2.5 Ground plan of Sangidas kuwa, *qasba* Phalodi

Figure 2.6 Showing slope of Sangidas kuwa, *qasba* Phalodi

Luniya Ka Kuwa

It is situated near Ranisar *talab* and is more than 350 feet deep. The water of this well is purely salty and was basically used in former times for people and animals both but later on only for animals.

Paramsukh Ka Kuwa

It was constructed by Paramsukh Rathi, a *baniya*[23]. It is 400-500 years old. It has now been fully closed for last 30 years. It also has four rectangular tanks. The depth of the well is more than 300 feet and could be operated by two sides (see Figure 2.7 & 2.8).

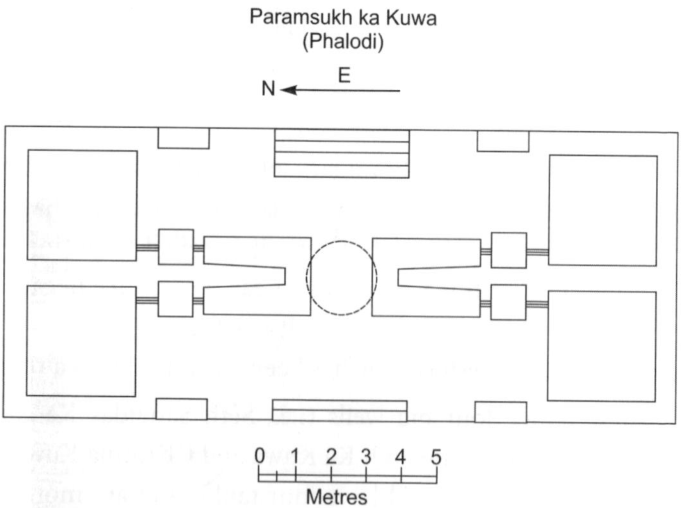

Figure 2.7 Plan of Paramsukh ka kuwa, *qasba* Phalodi

Figure 2.8 Paramsukh ka kuwa, *qasba* Phalodi

Chautina Kuwa

It is located within the boundary of brahmabagh and under the custody of a society. This well is also called Har Sagar. It is operated by four sides; therefore, it is called Chautina well. The water level of this well is quite near the surface because of its location in a depressed region. It has four square tanks. But presently tank of western side has been converted into a room.

These above four big wells (i.e., Seth Sangidas Ka Kuwa, Luniya Ka Kuwa, Paramsukh Ka Kuwa and Chautina Kuwa) are called *Kuwa* or *Kohar* and have four tanks, and are more than 360 feet deep[24].

KUWA/BERA/BERI

There are three types of wells: average deep well (upto 300 feet deep), *bera* (shallow but with one or more tanks) and *beri* (shallow well without a tank). Their details are as follows:

Dongron Ka Kuwa/Baniyo Ka Kuwa

It was constructed by a *baniya* and has two rectangular tanks. It is more than 400 years old and 300 feet deep. We have found *sati* inscription near the well. Water of the well is totally salty (see Figure 2.9 (a) & 2.9 (b).

Figure 2.9 (a) Dongron ka kuwa, *qasba* Phalodi

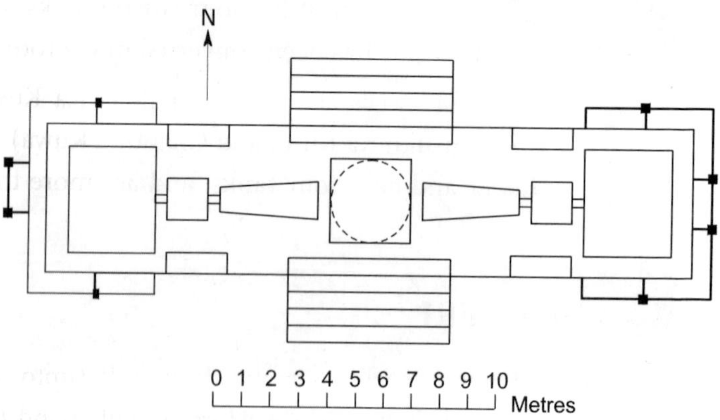

Figure 2.9 (b) Ground plan of Dongron ka kuwa, *qasba* Phalodi

Beris/beras (see Figure 2.10) were mostly excavated in and around the north of the *qasba* and *maliyon ka baas* because of the slope towards it (see Figure 2.3 & 2.4). Phalodi can see on the contour map and it can be explain that the centre of *qasba* Phalodi is 779 meters in its height from the sea level, while *maliyon ka baas* is less than 779 meters reducing to only 712 meters further north.The level continuously reduces towards the north of the *qasba*[25]. Many of the wells are situated in the Brahman's garden (*Brahman ki baghichi*) while 40 to 60 *beris* (small wells) are located in every part of agricultural land which were used for irrigating vast tract[26].

Dundiya Ka Bera

It is situated within the four walls of the garden (*bagichi*) of Dundi Brahmans. It is very old and has one side square tank. It was used to water garden-producing fruits and vegetables. (see Figure 2.10).

Figure 2.10 Dundiya ka bera, *qasba* Phalodi

Bohro Ki Beri

It is situated in the garden of Bohra Brahman. It is a shallow well (*kachcha kuwa*) without any tank and was used for gardening purposes. It is still being operated with the help of a tubewell (see Figure 2.11)

Figure 2.11 Bohron ki beri, *qasba* Phalodi

Thanviyon Ka Bera/Dani Rai Ka Bera

It is situated in the garden of Thanvi Brahman. It has two tanks. This well is also known as Dani Rai well and is counted among the big wells.

Jaypuriya Ki Beri

It is situated in the garden of Jaypuriyas which is under Jaypuriya Samaj. This well is without any tank.

Kallon Ki Beri

It is situated in the garden of Kalla Brahmans. This well is also without tank.

Vyason Ki Beri

It is situated in the garden of Vyas Brahmans and is not attached to any tank.

Joshiyon Ki Beri

It is situated in the garden of Joshi Brahmans and no tank is attached to it.

Guchiyon Ki Beri

It is situated in the garden of Guchiya Brahmans and no tank is attached to it.

BAORIS

Two *baoris* are also found in the *qasba*: one is called (*bhaiyyon ki baori*) which is situated within the boundary of the garden of *bhaiyya.* According to the locals, basically this structure belongs to the *baniya* caste, while in Bikaner region *bhaiyyas* belongs to the Kayasth community. Near this *baori* we found an old rectangular *beri* known as Latiyal well which is without any tank. The second *baori* is situated inside the Phalodi fort which was constructed with the fort itself.

TALAB/TALAI/NADI

Ranisar Talab

It is located on the north - east of the *qasba* of Phalodi. There is an inscription installed on the north-west facade of the tank.

According to this inscription it was constructed in VS 1589/ AD 1532 and is the oldest *talab* of the *qasba* (see Figure 2.13). It is reported by the experts (Brahmarshi H.K. Chhangani, 70 years old, and also a temple priest) that the *ghats* of this *talab* were constructed by a queen of this area. It is therefore, called Ranisar Talab. The date of the construction of the *ghats* is of later period and verified by the inscriptions which are attached with the *ghats*. The years of inscription are VS 1962/AD 1905 and VS 1985/AD 1928, respectively. This *talab* has two inlets to store the maximum rain water; one of them was also working as an outlet in case of overflow of water in the tank. Two *gaughat* can also be seen in this *talab*. Its main catchment area is spread upto village Ekagaon, 10 kms west from this *talab*. (see Figure 2.12 (a) & 2.12 (b) and Figure 2.13).

Figure 2.12 (a) Ranisar talab, *qasba* Phalodi

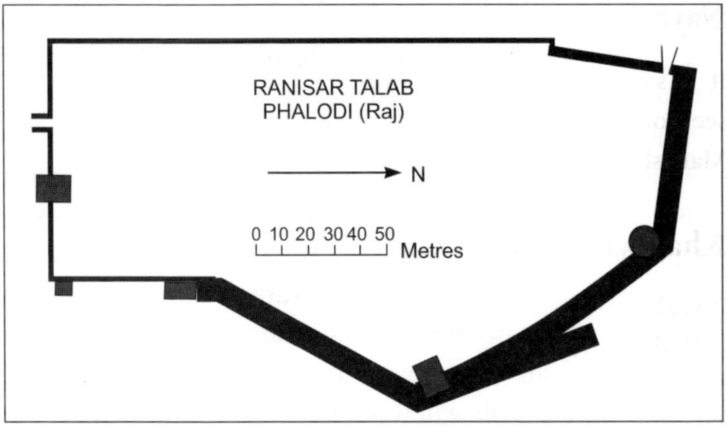

Figure 2.12 (b) Ground plan of Ranisar talab, *qasba* Phalodi

Figure 2.13 Inscription of Ranisar talab, *qasba* Phalodi

Seranad Talai

It was situated on the east of the *qasba* and presently it has lost its existence due to encroachment done by locals.

Naya Talab

It is situated in the south-west of the *qasba*. A *sarai* is also seen on the western bank of the tank. It was constructed by a Maheshwari *baniya.*

Khatriyo Ka Talab/Khatrinada

It is also situated in the south-west of the *qasba* and is attached with the Naya Talab.

Ramsar Talab

It is also situated in the south-west of the *qasba* and has two old inscriptions. One inscription has lost its date while another belongs to VS 1613/AD 1556. It is more than 50 feet deep, and attached to the above mentioned *talabs* i.e., Naya, and Khatrinada Talab. (see Figure 2.14 & 2.15).

Figure 2.14 Ramsar talab, *qasba* Phalodi

Figure 2.15 Inscription of Ramsar talab, *qasba* Phalodi (unreadable)

Chikhliya Talab

It is situated in the west of the *qasba*. Its *ghat* was constructed later on by a Maheshwari *baniya* in VS 1983/AD 1926. The original *talab* was more than 400 years old. Its main catchment area is in the west side, a *nallah (nadi)* passes through the east of this *talab,* called as *qila nadi*. Nainsi explain *bahlau* in his monumental work *Marwar-ra-pargana-ri-Vigat* and is called *nallah* (see Figure 2.16 & 2.17).

Figure 2.16 Chikhliya talab, *qasba* Phalodi

Figure 2.17 Nallah *(Bahlau)*, *qasba* Phalodi

Shivsar Talab

It is located at the west of the *qasba* and was constructed by a Pushtikar (*pushkarna*) Brahman and was dedicated to Lord Shiva.

Panniyari Nadi

It is very small and located in the west of the *qasba*. It was constructed by a Pushtikar Brahman.

Gulab Sagar

It is situated in the north-west of the *qasba* and has vast catchment area in its south-west. It has a *sarai* on the east of it[27] (see Figure 2.18). It is also very interesting to note that a *sarai* on the bank of the water body shows that this *qasba* later on emerged as a trading centre which is found in the archival records (see Appendix 2.3).

Figure 2.18 Showing *sarai* of Gulab Sagar, *qasba* Phalodi

II

RURAL WATER BODIES OF PHALODI

We have surveyed more than thirteen villages (*tehsil* Phalodi) for which we have sources, such as Muhnot Nainsi's *Marwar-ra-pargana-ri-Vigat*, *Phalodi bahi* of VS 1701/AD 1644 and other revenue records are available in Rajasthan State Archives, Bikaner[28]. The data collected through these fieldworks are given below:

VILLAGE MOKHERI

This village is located 8 kms south of *qasba* Phalodi. The village was colonized 600 years ago in VS 1515/AD 1458 by Mukheri, a Paliwal Brahman who immigrated from Pali. In our survey we found four *talabs*, and two wells. The crops raised in 1660's were *bajra, moth, til* and cotton. The last one was produced in large quantity. Its details are as follows:

Mokhorai Talab

This *talab* was dug by Mokhaji, a Brahman migrant from Pali. An inscription of VS 1556/AD 1499 is put on one side of the tank, and numerous *sati* memorial inscriptions are also there. The water of this tank is still in use. The slope of this village is towards *qasba* Phalodi and therefore the overflow of all the *talabs* and *talais* goes towards the *qasba*. A *sarai* is also constructed on the bank of the tank which shows that the village had its commercial significance and was connected with Phalodi town and located on trade junction[29]. It is quite possible that the crops were being sent to Phalodi market and from there to other parts of the state.

Jasolai Talab

It is located on the east of the village and was excavated by Jasraj, an Adigaur Brahman also a migrant from Pali. We have found an inscription of VS 1516/AD 1459 near the *talab.* The overflow of this *talab* goes to the Mokhelai talab and then it falls into Nahad Ki Nadi talai.

Nahad Ki Nadi

It is closely located towards the north of the village. The overflow of the *talai* runs towards north-east and joins Jasolai.

Bhramolai

It is located in the north of the village and was dug by Bhramoji.

Conclusively, we are able to say that the overflow of all the *talabs* and *talais* (*kachcha* - small pond) runs towards north of the village and falls into *nallah* (channel) of the *qasba* Phalodi.

Apart from this, we also found two wells (Purana kuwa and Naya kuwa). According to the experts of the area both wells were constructed along with the establishment of the village in AD 1458[30].

VILLAGE KHEECHAN

This village is located 4 kms on the east of the *qasba.* Here, we found six *talabs, talais* and a well, while Nainsi records four *talabs* in 1660's which means two water bodies were constructed later. Besides this, it also mentions twenty *beris* (shallow wells) in a *nadi* which was passing by the side of Kheechan, *nadi* has been explored by our survey team but *beris* could not be traced. Presently this village is a tourist destination.

Ratadi Nadi

It is located in the east of the village. It is still in use and known for the stay of Syberian birds locally known as *Kurjan.* This village is more than 450 years old.

Vijay Sagar Talab

It is situated near Ratadi Nadi and is still in use. It was dug by Vijaya Seth.

Kheechan Talab

It is a very big *talab* and known by its village name. It is also called as *nallah ke bagal ka talab.* The overflow irrigates a vegetable garden and then falls into a *nallah* (channel) passing through the west of the *talab*, and then again goes to its north-west and finally merges with the *qila nallah* which passes near *maliyon ka baas*[31].

Dhaul Ki Nadi

It is also situated near Kheechan talab and its overflow falls into this *nadi.*

Khatrinada Talab

It has lost its existence now, but its remains are still visible. A well Rathiyon ka kuwa is found in its vicinity. It was constructed by Rathi, a Maheshwari caste.

Our survey of this village shows that the slope of the village is towards west and north-west, therefore water goes in that direction.

VILLAGE MOHRA

This village is located 4 kms north of the *qasba* and here we found a *naadi* (*talab*) and a well (see Figure 2.19 and Figure 2.20(a) & 2.20(b). *Qila nadi* passes through this village and flows towards Malar and Bap,[32] etc.

Figure 2.19 Mohra gaon ka talab, *qasba* Phalodi

Figure 2.20 (a) Mohra gaon ka kuwa, *qasba* Phalodi

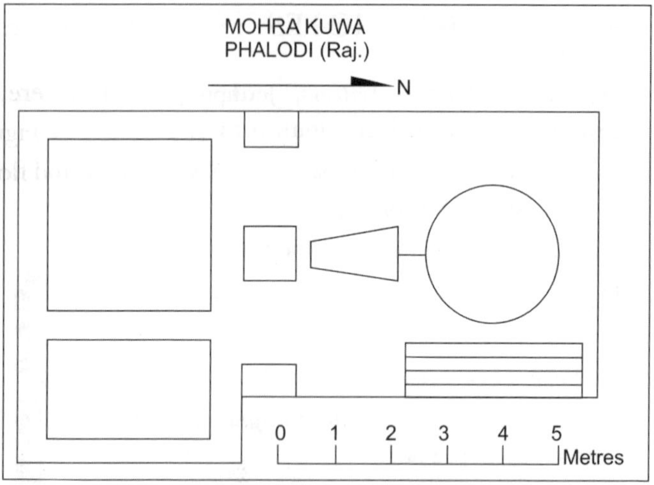

Figure 2.20 (b) Ground plan of Mohra gaon ka kuwa, *qasba* Phalodi

Moreover, a preliminary survey of ten villages belonging to the Paliwal Brahmans has also been conducted. The names of these villages are: Sabrij, Jaliwaro, Mokheri, Dahiya Kohar, Hupali, Chhila, Godhanli, Varnari. Naberi and Meha Kohar (attached with the *qasba).* The information about these villages is available in Nainsi's *Vigat*[33].

From the above evidence it appears that the people of Marwar (*qasba* Phalodi) successfully developed the techniques for irrigation and agricultural production in the area, which was otherwise suffering from the dearth of water. The information about the water bodies are adequately described in Nainsi's *Vigat.* From this evidence it emerges that the water-harvesting management of all these units were commendable. It is generally believed that the knowledge of the Paliwal Brahmans about the water-management was outstanding. They had developed their knowledge both about the surface as well as underground water management specifically in the desert tracts and built water bodies accordingly. In true sense they can be called men, having 'scientific knowledge' about water.

NOTES

1. *Rajasthan District Gazetteers*, Jodhpur, ed., B.D. Agrawal, Government of Rajasthan, Jaipur, 1979, p. 513.
2. *The Imperial Gazetteers of India*, Vol. XX, Today & Tomarrow's Printers, New Delhi, 1908, p. 128.
3. *Rajasthan District Gazetteers*, Jodhpur, op. cit., p.514.
4. Ibid.
5. Ibid.
6. *The Imperial Gazetteers of India*, Vol. XX, op. cit., p. 129.
7. Archibald Adams, *The Western Rajputana State*, second edition, London, 1900, p. 294.
8. Ibid.
9. Ibid.
10. *Bera* means shallow well with one or more tanks. Nainsi's *Vigat* recorded more than 300 *beras* in *qasba* Phalodi.
11. *Beri* means shallow well without tanks. Nainsi recorded more than 400 *beris* in *qasba* Phalodi. Sometimes ten feet deep sweet-water *beris* were also found.
12. Muhnot Nainsi, *Marwar –ra-pargana-ri-Vigat*, ed., Narain Singh Bhati, Vol-II, Jodhpur Rajasthan Prachya Vidya Pratishthan, Jodhpur, 1969, pp. 12-15.
13. *Vigat*-II, op. cit., pp. 12-36.
14. Field work.
15. Physical Survey of the site and conducted a series of interviews with the locals.
16. K.C.Jain, *Ancient Cities and Towns of Rajasthan*, Motilal Banarsidass, Delhi, 1972.
17. Ibid., pp. 13-15.
18. Ibid.
19. Ibid.
20. Survey of the sites.

21. Ibid.

22. This well has four tanks connected to the main well is situated in the centre. We have collected several informations regarding this well from the locals.

23. Survey of the sites. Engrossment of *baniyas* in the digging of wells and other water bodies show the centre as trade and commerce (see Appendix 2.3 Phalodi on trade routes).

24. Field work.

25. Mr. Faiz Habib,(Senior Cartographer, Centre of Advanced Study, Department of History, Aligarh Muslim University, Aligarh) prepared all the contour maps with the help of Inch Map and other Maps of Rajasthan.

26. Muhnot Nainsi also provided precious information regarding the shallow wells (*beris*) of *pargana* Phalodi.

27. *Sarai* on Gulab Sagar show the centre as trade and commerce. It was trader's halting place.Trader was also halting in the temples of Rajasthan. Therefore, every temple had atleast one water bodies (i.e. *talab, kuwa, kuin, baowri*) for drinking as well as ritual purposes.

28. Muhnot Nainsi's *Marwar-ra-pargana-ri-Vigat, Phalodi Bahi* of VS 1701/AD 1644.

29. Physical survey and conducted a series of interviews with the mahant and old persons of the area.

30. We do not have any original record. It is oral information, collected through interviews with the locals.

31. Physical survey of the site.

32. Ibid.

33. Muhnot Nainsi, *Marwar-ra-pargana-ri-Vigat*, ed., Narain Singh Bhati, Vol-II, Jodhpur Rajasthan Prachya Vidya Pratishthan, Jodhpur, 1969.

■■■

3

Technique of Irrigation and Agricultural Production in Nagaur

The district takes its name from its principal town Nagaur which is also its headquarters[1]. The origin of the name is uncertain but an old reference[2] is available which shows that this place was formerly known as Nagapura. It was one of the chief towns of Ananta-gochar which included the regions of Harsa and Shakhambhari[3]. It is situated in Jodhpur division and located between latitude 26°25′ and 27°40′ north and longitude 73°10′ and 75°15′ east[4]. The maximum length of the district from north to south is about 146 kms and its maximum breadth from east to west is about 229 kms[5]. It is a place of great antiquity[6]. It was known by various names such as Nagapura[7], Nagaura[8], Nagapattanam[9], Ahipura[10] and Bhujangansgara[11].

This chapter is mainly based on the physical survey of the site to study the techniques of irrigation and agricultural production in *qasba* Nagaur situated in Marwar. The surveys and studies of medieval irrigational works in Rajasthan were done by some scholars as has already been explained in the Introduction. Therefore, we shall proceed to investigate various methods of water-harvesting in different localities. Contemporary

documents for *qasba* Nagaur[12] were consulted which form the baseline for our physical survey of the irrigational works. In the *qasba*, we explored surface as well as ground-water bodies[13]. Some of the *talabs* of *qasba* Nagaur have less deep wells called *beris*[14] in their beds. In this regard, we (author and the survey team) consulted many records and also met many experienced persons and eldermen at the survey sites, and came to know about seven *talabs* lying either in destroyed or in polluted form. Of these, Ginani *talab* is located inside the city wall and the rest are outside the wall. The *talabs* which still maintained their identity are few. Some of them receive aid from the state government for regular repair work. Water of these *talabs* is still being used only for drinking purposes for animals or other things by the local population. More or less the catchment areas of these *talabs* have been destroyed owing to the construction of residential buildings in its *agor*.

According to a survey conducted by Gairrick and demonstrated by us, there are altogether seven tanks at Nagaur. The existing water structure could become a good source of potable water and need immediate attention. They are also feeding a large number of wells and step-wells. The details of the surveyed sites especially the Shakkar talab, a source of irrigation for the agricultural land with the use of lifting system are mentioned below.

Shakkar Talab

Akbar left Ajmer and started his journey towards Nagaur after praying at the *dargah* of Khwaja Moinuddin Chishti on November 3, 1570 (Friday 4 *jamadiul akhir*, H. 978)[15]. After journeying for 12 consecutive days he finally reached Nagaur on November 15,

1570 (Wednesday 15 *jamadiul akhir,* H. 978)[16] (see Figure 3.1). He was welcomed at Nagaur by Khan-i Kalan Mir Mohammad who also organized a lunch (*bhoj*) in his respect[17]. The emperor participated at his *bhoj* and amply gifted him. Meanwhile, emperor saw a *talab.* The people of the area requested the emperor Akbar that the affluence and happiness of the villages of Nagaur depends on these three *talabs,* whereas one of them is Kayadaani, presently called as Gilani or Ginani talab.[18] Akbar issued an order to clean and renovate all the water structures of the *qasba.* Later on Ginani tank was reconstructed by Raja Rai Singh Rathore, elder son of Rao Amar Singh Rathore[19]. Second *talab* which was repaired on the order of Akbar was Shamsi talab[20], and thirdly, the Shakkar talab, originally known as the Kukkur talab was also cleaned and renovated[21]. The Shakkar talab has its own history which is explained in details by M.H. Siddiqui in his book on Nagaur[22]. We surveyed this *talab* and the other monuments which are built on the bank of this very large tank (see Figure 3.2 (a), & 3.2 (b), Figure 3.3, 3.4 and 3.5).

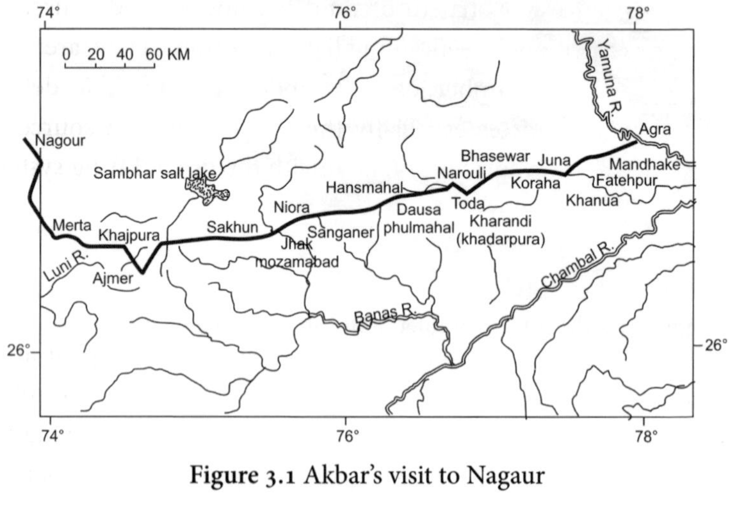

Figure 3.1 Akbar's visit to Nagaur

Figure 3.2 (a) Deepest view of the Shakkar talab, *qasba* Nagaur

Figure 3.2 (b) A view of inlet of the Shakkar talab, *qasba* Nagaur

Figure 3.3 A view of the main road separating the talab

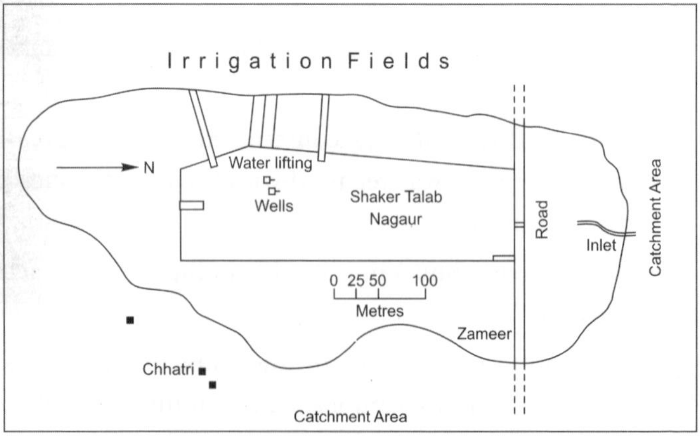

Figure 3.4 The Shakkar talab, *qasba* Nagaur

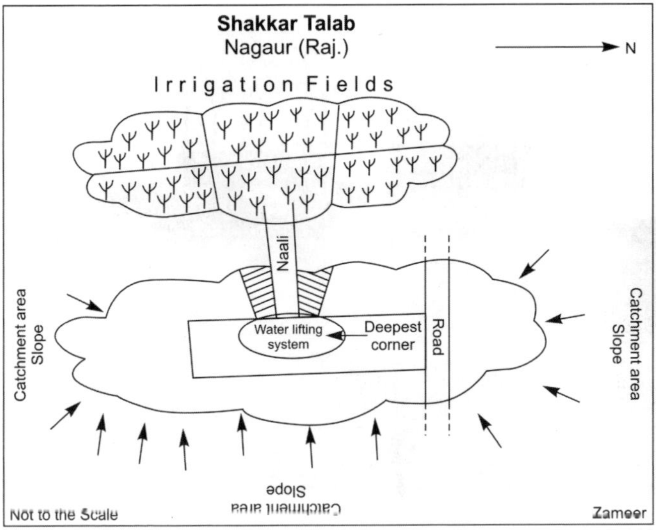

Figure 3.5 Showing slopes from *agor* towards the *talab* and the use of water from the Shakkar talab to irrigate fields

After the survey of this *talab* we are able to give an explanation as below:

- Initially this *talab* was constructed in the depression area; later on it was repaired with the use of stones and bricks around it.
- A new road connecting it with Jodhpur passes across the tank.
- Cenotaphs are also seen on the banks of *talab*. Near it two slabs with inscriptions are also found. One of them is of VS 1666/AD 1609 (see Figure 3.6 & 3.7).

Figure 3.6 Inscription near a cenotaph on the bank of the Shakkar talab

Figure 3.7 Full view of inscription

- Two metalled-wells are constructed on the bed of the south side of the tank. (see Figure 3.8)

Figure 3.8 Two wells on the bed of the Shakkar talab

- South-west corner is the deepest portion of the tank. Water was being lifted from this side for which a 50 ft. high wall was constructed. A metalled *naali* is constructed just in the mid of the raised wall which flows towards the agricultural lands. (see Figure 3.9, 3.10 & 3.11).

Figure 3.9 Metalled wall of the talab

Figure 3.10 Metalled *naali* of the talab

Figure 3.11 Agricultural lands near the talab

- There are two main sources to store water in this tank from the slope on two sides. One was the overflow coming from the Nada talab from south of the tank; second was a slope from west side from where the water flowed into the tank[23].

It is essencial to clarify here that the general perceptions of the locals are very clear about the use of water, especially in desert areas where water is scarce. Shyamal Das, the author of the *Vir Vinod,* raises a question about a well and canal irrigation especially in the Mewar region. He writes that there was no system of agricultural irrigation about 200 years ago. That is why except the wells for drinking water and for irrigating the gardens, there were no signs to show that agricultural fields were also irrigated in the past. No canals were even dug out from the tanks. According to B. L. Bhadani the above statement of Shyamal Das is not based on facts because it is negated by the extant evidence[24]. A work of B.L. Bhadani and Jibraeil proved that the wells and *talabs* were being used earlier also for the irrigation purposes in the desert areas of Rajasthan[25].

Generally two types of water-lifting devices appear to have been in operation. One was *charas* (leather-bucket) and the second was *rahat* (Persian wheel). According to B.L. Bhadani, the *charas* was employed on the wells of the *parganas* located in the east and north, while the *rahat* was used in the areas of the south and the western parts of the state. This means that the water level was nearer to the surface in the east and north of the state, while the south and the western part contained water at considerably a lower depth[26]. In our survey of the *qasba* Nagaur, we explored a *talab* (Shakkar talab explained above) which was being used for irrigation operated by the *charas*[27].

Through this study it appears that the people of the *qasba* Nagaur (Marwar) had successfully developed techniques for irrigation and agricultural production in an area which was erstwhile facing an acute dearth of water.

NOTES

1. *Rajasthan District Gazetteers,* Nagaur, ed., K.K.Sehgal, Government of Rajasthan, Jaipur, 1975, p.1.
2. Dashrath Sharma, ed. *Rajasthan Through the Ages,* Vol. I, Rajasthan State Archives, Bikaner, 1966, p.17. Tod also mentions that the Rathors conquered Nagaur or Nagdurg (the serpent's castle) from the Mohils, who held fourteen hundred and forty villages as late as the fifteenth century. See James Tod, *Annals and Antiquities of Rajasthan,* Vol. III, Humphrey Milford, Oxford University Press, London, 1920, p.1449, fn.4. *The Imperial Gazetteer of India,* 1908, Vol. XVIII, mentions that the town is said to have taken its name from its traditional founders, the Naga Rajputs.
3. *Rajasthan District Gazetteers,* Nagaur, op. cit., p.1.
4. Ibid. (*qasba* Nagaur lies in the latitude 27°12′ N and longitude 73°44′ E).
5. Ibid.
6. K.C. Jain, *Ancient Cities and Towns of Rajasthan,* Motilal Banarsidass, Delhi, 1972, p. 242.
7. Ibid., Cf, RB, I, p.47.
8. Ibid., Cf, GOS, LXXVI, p.156.
9. Ibid., Cf, *Ashtalakshi Prasasti,* published in JSP, XVI, p.16.
10. Ibid., Cf. PR, II, pp. 54-55.
11. Ibid., Cf. ONS, p. 19.
12. This *qasba* was surveyed under a project, sanctioned by Mehrangarh Museum Trust, Jodhpur, by the author of this book.
13. In our survey we explored many water bodies comprising eight *talabs*, four *baoris* and many wells in *qasba* Nagaur.
14. It is small well in the bed of *talabs* (lakes). See the *Dying Wisdom, Rise, Fall and Potential of India's Traditional Water Harvesting*

System, eds., Anil Agarwal and Sunita Narain, reprint, CSE, Delhi, 2005, p.389 (Glossary). *Beris* stand for shallow wells without tanks. Nainsi recorded more than 400 *beris* in the *qasba* Phalodi. Sometimes ten feets deep, sweet-water *beris* were also found in Muhnot Nainsi. See *Marwar – ra-pargana-ri-Vigat*, ed., Narain Singh Bhati, Vol-II, Jodhpur Rajasthan Prachya Vidya Pratishthan, Jodhpur, 1969 (Chapter on the *qasba* Phalodi). Also see B.L. Bhadani and Jibraeil, *Techniques of Irrigation in the Desert area of Phalodi in Medieval Times*, Proceeding of the *Rajasthan History Congress*, Bikaner, 2008, pp.36-43.

15. M.H.Siddiqui, *Madhya Kaleen Nagaur Ka Itihas*, Maharaja Mansingh Pustak Prakash, Jodhpur, 2001, pp.83-84.
16. Ibid.
17. Ibid.
18. Other two *talabs* were Shams and Kukur (latter Shakkar). The people of the area also known as pleadedy to the emperor that many of the people migrated from their houses who were living near these *talabs* due to scarcity of water as almost all these tanks got filled up by the sands.
19. M.H.Siddiqui, *Madhya Kaleen Nagaur ka Itihas*, op. cit., pp.273-74.
20. Ibid.p. 84.
21. Ibid.
22. Ibid. [Nagaur was an important trading centre in Marwar, exporting different varieties of goods, food grains, minerals, etc., and importing needed goods from different towns of Rajasthan, India and even overseas. It was also a big centre where blended of various cultures with Sufi centres and Jain temples raising the values of the town. For details see Ghan Shyam Lal Devra , *A Study of the Trade Relations between Rajasthan and Sindh-Multan (AD 1650-1800)*, a chapter in his edited book *Socio-Economic History of Rajasthan*, Shri Jagdish Singh Gahlot, Research Institute Jodhpur, 1980; Jibraeil, '*Qasba* Nagaur : A Centre of Trade and Commerce During Delhi Sultanate', in a seminar proceeding *Re-Interpretating History of the Delhi Sultanate*, ed.,

Ali Athar, Woodpecker Publication and Publication Division, Aligarh Muslim University, Aligarh, First Edition-2014, pp. 31- 48; Jibraeil, '*Qasba* Nagaur: A Centre of Cultural Heritage of Medieval Rajasthan', in Felicitation Volume *Essayas in Indian History and Culture,* Idarah-I Adviyat-I Delli, New Delhi, 2013, pp.92-123.]

23. Physical survey of the site.
24. B.L.Bhadani, *Water Harvesting, Conservation and Irrigation in Mewar (AD 800 - 1700),* Manohar, Delhi, 2012, p. 26.
25. B.L.Bhadani and Jibraeil, 'Techniques of Irrigation in the Desert area of Phalodi in Medieval Times', Proceedings of *Rajasthan History Congress*, Bikaner, 2008, pp.36-43; and 'Water Harvesting and Techniques of Irrigation in Urban areas during Medieval Period: A Case Study of Bikaner', in a seminar proceeding *Urbanization and Trade Routes of Rajasthan*, ed., S.P. Vyas, Book Treasure, Jodhpur, 2011, pp. 64 - 77.
26. B.L.Bhadani, *Water Harvesting, Conservation and Irrigation in Mewar (AD 800 - 1700),* op. cit., p. 26.
27. Physical survey of the site.

■■■

4

Water Bodies and Harvesting Techniques in Bikaner

The people of Bikaner developed techniques to harvest rain water which was some times used to grow vegetables in small areas, particularly situated near water bodies[1]. In this chapter an attempt is made to explore the water bodies of Bikaner and their harvesting technique. It is interesting to note that before settling down in the area, Rao Bika dispatched an advance party of "knowledgeable persons" to survey the area and find out a suitable place for the establishment of a headquarter for the new Rathor state in the northern part of the desert of present Rajasthan. His expert representatives first camped on the bank of a tank known as the Kodamdesar (see Appendix 4.1) from where they made an extensive survey of the area and found a suitable site. The expert perhaps chose this site because of the availability of tracts of *mudiya kankar*, which possesses excellent run off characteristics. This became the determining factor for the establishment of the new city (see Figure 4.1(a) and 4.1(b) it was founded in AD 1488, and was named Bikaner after the clan leader Rao Bika.[2]

It is the only city in the district and is located almost in its centre. It lies between 28°01′ latitude and 71°54′ and 73°19′ longitude. The city is situated on somewhat elevated ground at a height of about 232 metres above the mean sea level[3]. Formerly it was a walled city, but with changing times this wall lost its significance and its maintenance became unnecessary. Due to the growth of the population the city outgrew the wall and new colonies and buildings were constructed outside it [4].There are five entrances in the city wall called Kote gate, Jassusar gate, Nathusar gate, Seetala gate and Goga gate. Besides this, there were eight sally ports; some of these are *Hammalon-ki-bari* (the potter's gate), *Uston-ki-bari* (the builder's gate), *Kasaion-ki-bari* (the butcher's gate), *Pabu bari* and *Idgah bari* [5].

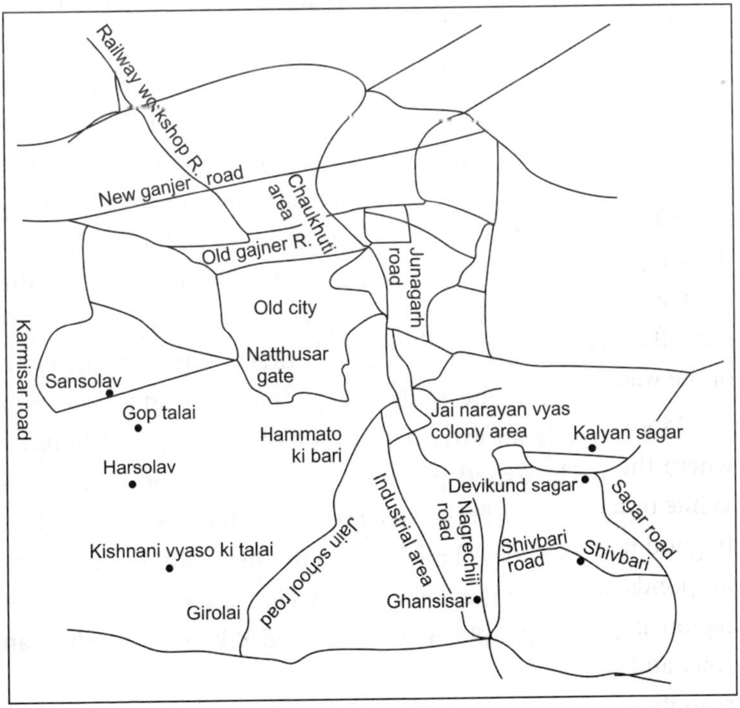

Figure 4.1 (a) Locality of Bikaner city

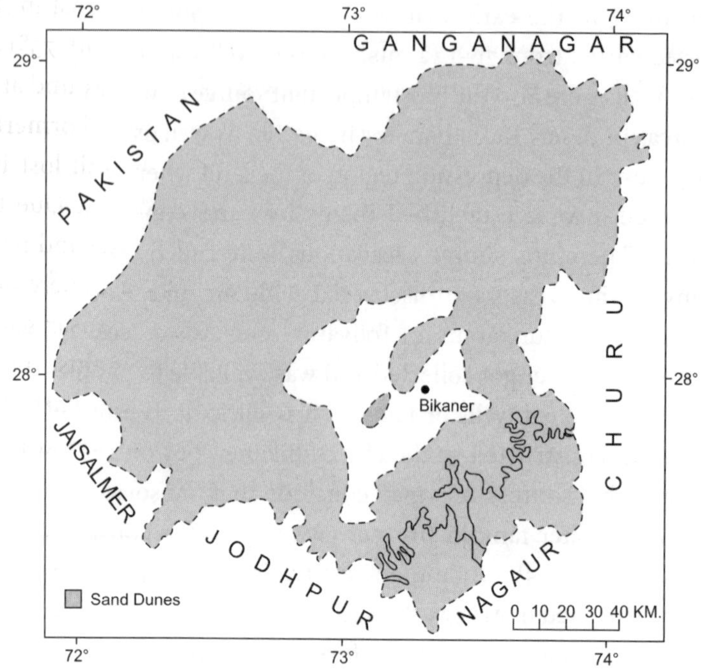

Figure 4.1(b) Outline map of Bikaner city

With an average rainfall ranging from 12.70 cm to 25.40 cm., there is practically no surface run off and therefore, no river worth the name.[6] There are, however, a few local *nallah* in which a little run off from the surface wherever it is hard, finds its way. Some of the water in these *nallah* is impounded in tanks for irrigation.[7]

More or less, the area of Bikaner, comes under the desert, where the possibility of involvement in agriculture is very less. While by and large, land use in the Thar is dependent on rainfall. In good rainfall years, large areas are cropped; rain water is stored in ponds, and underground tanks. Cultivation in the desert region is poor and precarious, though some tracts have better soils and are more productive. Irrigation is limited due to the scarcity of water in the west of the desert, and had traditionally been restricted to deep wells and rain water-harvesting system.

According to the early British Gazetteers' report the wells that existed varied from 76-122 mts, and one well was as deep as 150 mts.[8] Wells were also the most important source of water in almost all areas of desert Rajasthan, for irrigation as well as for drinking purposes.[9] In the depression region of the land where water could be stored, people established themselves and constructed their houses. Therefore, simple excavations were called '*sar*' *(sir)* and many of the areas were discovered with *sar*, like Kodamdesar, Norangdesar, Lunkaransar, Toliyasar and Adsar, etc. In such depressions water got collected and was available to people; these came to be called wells or *talabs*.[10] It is difficult to point out the first *talab* constructed in the city of Bikaner, but on the basis of the available sources one may conclude that Sansolao talab was the oldest water tank in Bikaner city, which was constructed in VS 1572/AD 1515[11] while the latest *talab* Kukh Sagar (Gindolai) was constructed in AD 1937[12]. According to a source total number of *talabs* in Bikaner was around forty[13]. However, it is not correct, because today we can count about sixty nine of them including the *taals* and *talais*. [14] (see Appendix 4.2).

P.W. Powlett mentions the name of the *talabs* in his work *Tanks of Bikaner* such as; Jassolai, Kharnada, Gogeji ki talai, Farsolai, etc., within the city wall, and out of it are Sur sagar, Bakhat sagar, Sansolao, Harsolao, Moondharo ka talab, Modiyon ka talab, etc.[15] In VS 1763/AD 1706, Udaychand Matheran also mentions the name of the six main *talabs* of Bikaner city in his 'Bikaner Ghazal' such as; Sur sagar, Gogeji ka talai, Savalakhi talai, Gharseesar, Sansolao and Harsolao.[16]

Prior to 1897, there was no special irrigation system in Bikaner. The erstwhile rulers of the state built the 'Gaggar Canal System' for irrigation, and tanks to store water for irrigation[17]. Rural and urban people used rain water, collected it in covered pits or *kund* (small pits-*kundi*) or simple excavations called *sar*,

where the ground was hard. Most places (villages also) in the desert tract had small ponds, and in a good season, there was sufficient water to drink for 7 to 8 months. If rainfall failed, then water was available for only 4 to 6 months and people had to bring water from the other villages, 20-30 kms. away[18].

Almost all water bodies were made by the erstwhile rulers, Jagirdars, and chieftains were reserved for their personal use. The people largely had to fend for themselves. Some of the water bodies were reserved for the use of the nobility while some others were used by the local populace. In few areas water bodies were also reserved for specific purposes (rituals) and the people were not allowed to use it even for drinking[19]. The local people also created numerous water bodies. In Rajasthan, there were various traditional water resource systems, namely *nadi*, *talab*, *johad*, *bandha*, *sagar*, *samand* and *sarovar* just to name a few.[20]

So when an average villager talks about a *nadi* they have a clear idea of what is being referred to, how water is collected in a *nadi*, how the area has been selected, how the *agor* (catchment) has been prepared, and what are the ground rules which govern the *agor*. At the digging, people would have a fair knowledge of the geological parameters of the area[21]. Similarly, while talking about a *talab*, the people of the region described the difference between a *talab* and a *nadi*. It is not merely the water capacity of a particular system which determines these terms but the way they are constructed and is what sort of natural conditions do they exists.[22]

Wells are another important source of water. There are different types of wells in Rajasthan. A *kuwa* (well) is usually owned by an individual. But there are larger wells known as *kohar* which is owned by the community. Then there are step-wells too known as *baoris* and some times *jhalaras*. *Baoris* usually have a religious significance and were constructed as a

philanthropic deed for *punya*. The structure and architectural pattern of a *jhalaras* is different from that of a *baori*.[23] People of rural and urban areas also dig *beris* (shallow and narrow wells) about 68 meters deep to collect sweet water. These *beris* provide drinking water for both human beings and livestock. *Beris* were also dug in the 'dry bed' of a river or a lake or a tank.[24] There are certain wells in Bikaner city known as Mohato ka kuwa and Acharyon ka kuwa having enormous quantities of water. These wells are about 300 fts deep with slim chances of drying up. Water-harvesting, its distribution and its use were regulated by the community. Before the onset of monsoon the *agor* or *payton* (catchment) of the tanks would be methodically cleaned of all waste and rubbish. Labour for this was contributed by all beneficiaries. Similarly, for desiltation of tanks, labour was contributed by the entire community.[25]

The decision to establish Bikaner as an urban centre seems to have been strongly influenced by the availability of tracts of *mudiya kankar*[26], possesses with excellent run off characteristics that facilitated rain-water harvesting through an elaborate network of tanks. The catchment areas (*agors*) of these tanks were treated as a sacred passage where human activities like defection were prohibited. Normally, the catchment areas, some of which were quite extensive, were kept well-wooded. In towns around Bikaner, there were abundant tanks. The more important ones being Kolayat with a catchment area with 14,900 hectares, Gajner with 12,950 hectares and Ganga sarovar with 7,950 hectares. The water needs of the town were met by the innumerable tanks in and around Bikaner, together with the wells and *kunds* that each house traditionally built for harvesting rain-water from the rooftops[27]. The water from the tanks was used mainly for drinking purposes. If in any year there was less than normal rainfall and the tanks did not get filled, water from nearby wells and tanks would be obtained, to fill the household tanks. In this way, the people of Bikaner were able to meet their water requirements.[28]

At the turn of century, Bikaner had more than forty old tanks (see Figure 4.2). Today except for Harsolao, the catchment areas of almost all the tanks have been destroyed[29]. Some of the old tanks like the Jasolai, Baghinada and Rangolai have been wiped off the map of Bikaner. In their place housing colonies have comes up.[30]

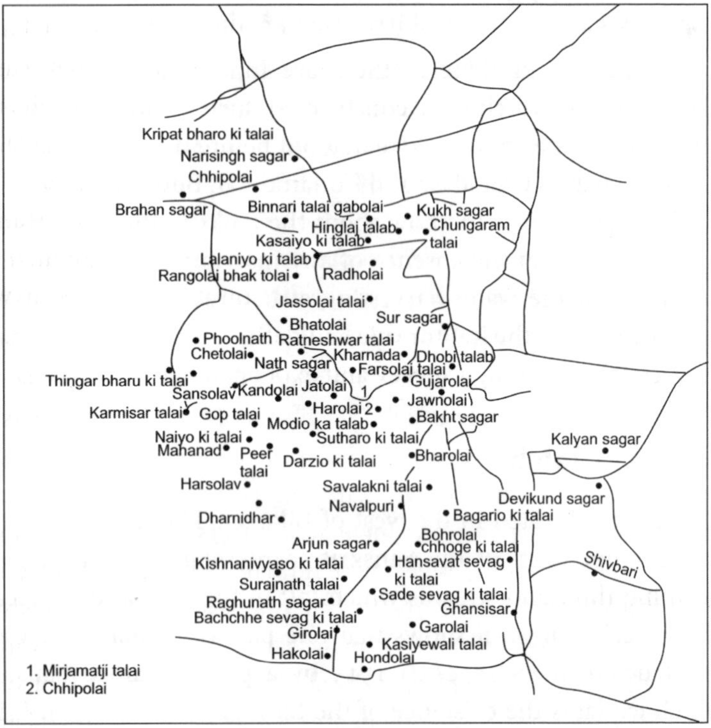

Figure 4.2 Tanks of Bikaner city

For drinking purposes, every house in Bikaner also had *tankas* (tanks-*kund*). These were built inside the main house or in the courtyard. In addition, tanks and wells in large number fulfil the requirement of the city dwellers. But due to the Rajasthan canal, plenty of water is now available in the town. Therefore, people do not feel the need for traditional *tankas*, leading to a decline in the use of tank-water known as *palar pani* (rain-water).

In the light of above, an effort has been made to study the methods and techniques adopted by the people to harvest water and utilize it both for drinking as well as irrigation purposes. This study is based on the physical survey supplemented by the archival and non-archival sources. First, the methods of water-harvesting systems and modes are taken up, and then the techniques and methods of irrigation are discussed.

In the city of Bikaner, there are innumerable tanks (see Appendix 4.2) which were constructed during a long course of time. Some water-bodies were dug out before the coming of the Rathors, such as Chandsar and Kodamdesar. Besides this, we do not have any means to know about the tanks in the pre-Rathor period because of the absence of any inscription or document. But some of the water-harvesting structures erected after the establishment of the Rathor rule had definite evidence which has been collected through survey and explained below in details.

Sansolao Talab

This tank is located in the west of Bikaner. The term Sansolao is a corrupt form of the Sanskrit word *sahashralao* probably meaning thousand streams which fall in together at one place. The inscription on it shows that one part (*tat=ghat*) of it was constructed in VS 1572/AD 1515 by a person named Sansoji which explains the existence of the tank prior to this year. It is believed that it got constructed by the grandson of Saloji. People involved in the erection of this water-body were Maheshwaris by caste who had their ancestory in the city of Bikaner. It was designed in a systematic way to tap the run-off water from three directions. In the middle of it, there is a cenotaph (*chhatri*) which is now in dilapidated condition. The length of this *talab* is around 105 meters and the breadth is about 70 meters. It is said that originally it was 20-25 feet deep but now the depth has

reduced because of the silt collected over the years. (see Figure 4.3 & 4.4). Now its catchment area is being encroached upon and the tank is gradually losing its past glory. The original *agor* was more than 350 *bighas* and it had approximately 10 *ghats* including a *gau* and a *paniyar ghat*.[31]

Figure 4.3 Sansolao talab (Bikaner city)

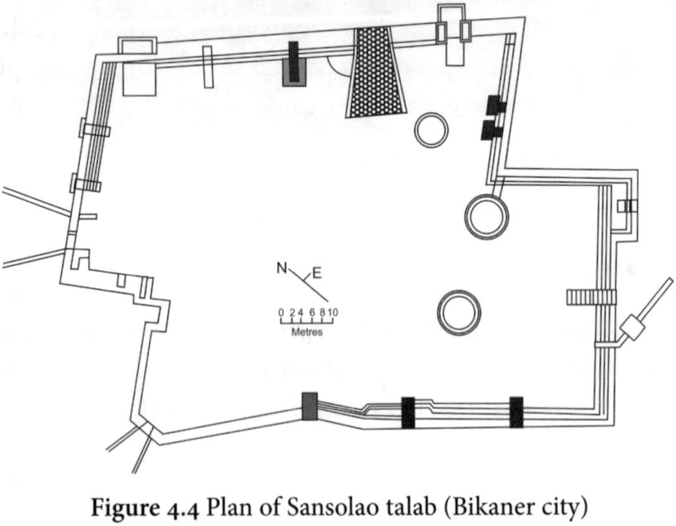

Figure 4.4 Plan of Sansolao talab (Bikaner city)

Devi-Kund Sagar

Ridmalsar Purohitan near Bikaner is also known as Devi-Kund Sagar (see Figure 4.5). It was constructed during the period of Rai Singh (1541 to 1612), who was the first to make alliance with the Mughal emperor Akbar. Devi-Kund Sagar is about 280 metres long and 117 metres broad. It is situated 5 miles east of the city.[32] The area around it got developed into a village which came to be known as Sagar gaon[33].

Figure 4.5 Devi-kund sagar (Bikaner city)

Kalyan Sagar

In the vicinity of the Devi-kund sagar another tank Kalyan sagar was excavated by the rulers of Bikarner. Probably it came into existence in VS 1630/AD 1573 after the death of Maharaja Kalyan Singh (see Figure 4.6).

Figure 4.6 Kalyan sagar (Bikaner city)

It was near the graveyard of the royal family. The ruler Rao Kalyan Singh mentioned about its beautiful cenotaphs near the *talab* to Maharaja Dungar Singh.[34] This sagar had a vast catchment area but it was probably meant to be used by the ruling family alone. But entire area of sagar benefited from these two tanks because they had raised the water table almost close to the surface. The 365 memorials of the rulers of Bikaner and their consorts surround the sagar, making it esquisitely beautiful. Children of the royal family and their close relatives have also found a place among those memorials (see Figure 4.7). Most of the memorials are built in white marble and red stones of Dulmera[35]. The earliest *chhatri* is of Rai Kalyanmal (AD 1542-AD 1571) and the last is of Karni Singh[36]. It is interesting to note that paintings appears for the first time in the *chhatri* of Ratan Singh (AD 1828-AD 1851) and then they continue in the later ones; the best one adorns the *chhatri* of Maharaja Ganga Singh (1887-1943)[37].

Figure 4.7 *Chhatri* near Kalyan sagar

Shivbari Talab

It was earlier located on the south-east outskirt of the city but now with the expansion of the city it forms part of it. It appears that this tank existed since time immemorial because of a deep depression on the site. But present brickline structure was constructed by Maharaja Dungar Singh in the memory of his father. Along with the tank, a temple complex of Lord Shiva was also raised; therefore, the entire area came to be known as Shivbari[38]. Its catchment is located in the north and the area is quite vast. The land of this direction is of *mudiya kankar*. So entire water rushes towards this depression and raises the water level of the surrounding area. Nowadays its *agor* has been lost and there is no possibility of the tank filling up with water. Therefore, the area of the tank is being utilized as the playground by the children of the region[39] (see Figure 4.8 & 4.9).

Figure 4.8 Shivbari talab (Bikaner city)

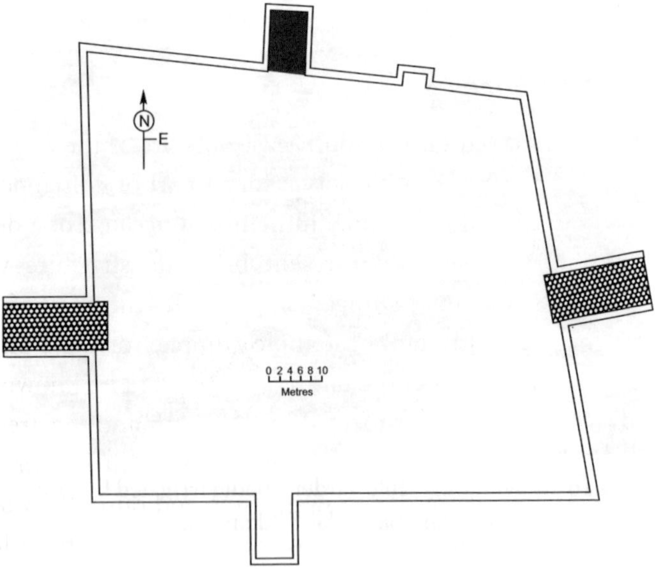

Figure 4.9 Plan of Shivbari talab (Bikaner city)

As narrated above the water level of the area had reached quite close to the surface. Consequently, two wells were excavated to tap sub-soil water. These wells were employed to irrigate small plots of land where vegetables were grown. These wells are mentioned below:

Juniya Well

Adjacent to Shivbari talab, there is a green belt where a large number of trees are standing. There, we found a well (*kuwa*) known as Juniya kuwa (old well) which was used for irrigation. It is still in operation. Now its mouth is covered with iron rods and a pumping machine has been installed there[40] (see Figure 4.10).

Figure 4.10 Showing vegetable gardens being irrigated by Juniya well near Shivbari talab (Bikaner city)

Sagariya Well

According to the inhabitants of the area, a well has also been constructed near that region called Sagariya kuwa. It is so named because it provides continuous supply of water for irrigation as well as and drinking purposes[41] (see Figure 4.11).

Figure 4.11 Sagariya well near Shivbari talab (Bikaner city)

Lakeshwar Baori

In front of Shivbari talab a beautiful temple exists wherein two beautiful *baoris* were constructed known as Lakeshwar and Kakeshwar *baori* whose water was utilized for religious rituals and other mundane purposes[42] (see Figure 4.12).

Figure 4.12 Lakeshwar baori (Bikaner city)

Phoolnath Talab

Formerly, it was called as Raghunath sagar. It was named after a person called Raghunath Mundhara in whose memory it was constructed by his family members in VS 1777/AD 1720. Therefore, it is also called Mundhara talab. Later on a saint Phoolnath came and sat there in deep meditation; therefore, people also started calling it Phoolnath talab.[43]

This tank is unique because it possesses characteristics of a tank as well as that of a *baori*. It receives rain-water and also tapes underground water. In its bottom there is a step-well which receives sub-soil water. It contains about 22 steps to reach to the water level. It is 84 metres in length and 54 metres in breadth[44]. In the middle of the catchment area (*agor*) there is a *kund* on the hilltop (a kind of water-harvesting structure) which receives rain-water. When it gets filled up the surplus water goes into the

tank through a channel (*nallah/nali*) constructed specifically for this purpose. This is still in operation[45] (see Figure 4.13 & 4.14).

Figure 4.13 *Baori* inside the Phoolnath talab (Bikaner city)

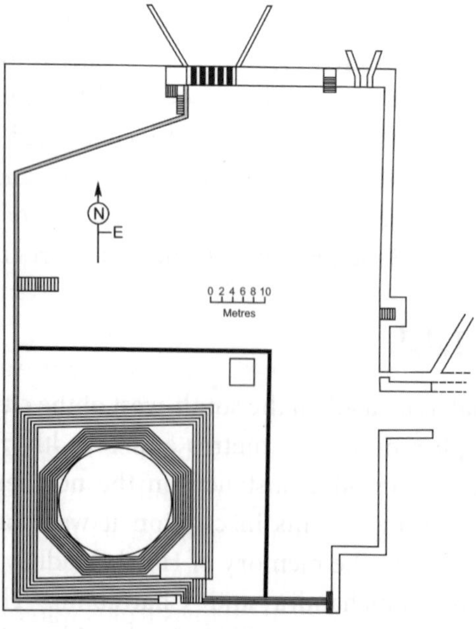

Figure 4.14 Plan of Phoolnath talab, (Bikaner city)

Ghadsisar Talab

This tank is located on the south of the city of Bikaner. It was constructed in VS 1745/AD 1688, which is verified by the *lekha and jama kharach bahi* of VS 1745-48/AD 1688-91 (s.no.20 *bahi* no.55), Rajasthan States Archives, Bikaner[46]. Later on, an extensive repair work was carried out by Seth Ram Lal alias Hakuji Baghari in VS 1955/AD 1898. It is reported by a local knowledgeable person Mangi Lal Swami (80 years old) that before the construction of this tank, there existed a small tank (*talai*) [47].

It had a vast catchment (*agor*) area and was well maintained when it was in use. But gradually most of the area was encroached upon for the construction of the buildings, and local industries also grew up. Therefore, the north of the tank (*agor*) is presently known as industrial and Bara bazaar region. The west side of it has a *gaughat* (drinking place for cattle) and other *ghats* in different sides are still in existence.[48]

Interesting information emerged after our two consecutive fieldworks. We discovered the outlet of the tank is located on the southern direction. The overflow goes towards south and south-west, where there is an open space which is used for growing vegetables by the members of the *Mali* community and supplied to whole the city. We have taken detailed measurement of the structure which comes to 118 metres in length and 100 metres in breadth.[49]

Harsolao Talab

Harsolao talab is located on the south-west of the city of Bikaner, with its length around 115 metres and breadth 73 metres. It has a Sanskrit inscription installed on the northern facade of the tank. According to this inscription it was constructed in VS 1681/AD 1624 in the memory of Harsh Madhav by his three sons: Kalyan, Ramchandra and Chatrabhuj. The deceased belonged to the Harsh caste, a *Pushtikar* (*pushkarna*) Brahmin[50].

It has a vast catchment (*agor*) area which is well maintained even today by a trust. It is reported by local person who has knowledge of this that some time back a small tank (*talai*) was in existence in the catchment area, but now it has vanished. The water-body is surrounded by hill tracts of *mudiya kankar* which possesses excellent run off characteristics. The entire catchment area is made of this material (see Figure 4.15 & 4.16).

Figure 4.15 Harsolao talab (Bikaner city)

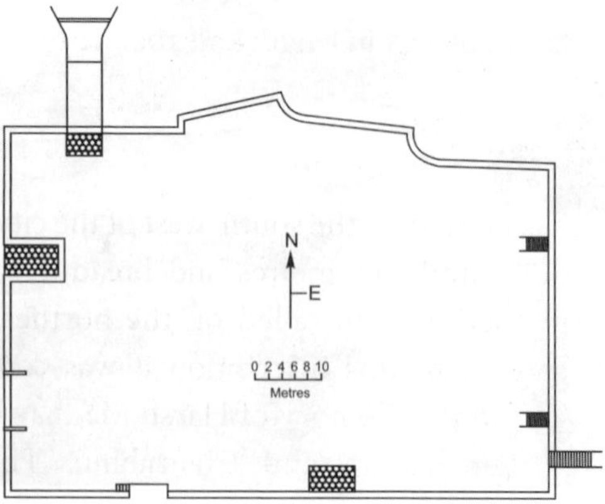

Figure 4.16 Plan of Harsolao talab (Bikaner city)

WELLS

Mohton Ka Kuwa

This well is situated in the south of the Sansolao talab which is located in the west of Bikaner, and the effect of this tank is also visible in the Acharyon ka kuwa. It is operated from a single side, i.e., in the west but presently it is not operational. On one corner of the well a cenotaph (*chhatri*) was raised and below it there is a chamber probably for the well-operator. It is said that the well is more than 350 feet deep. There is an inscription of later period (VS 1956/AD 1899) on a red sand stone slab (*thambh*) which also depicts a figure of a snake on one side and the name of its builder with date on the other side[51] (see Figure 4.17 & 4.18)

This well receives water from an underground current connected with the adjacent Sansolao tank. Local people call it an underground *nadi,* i.e., river. The water had percolated from the tank, ran through the stream and was taped by digging the well. Its length is 22.30 metres and breadth comes to 11.40 metres. The location, size, architecture and a view can be seen in the following plan (see Figure 4.19).

Figure 4.17 Mohton ka kuwa (Bikaner city)

Figure 4.18 Symbol of a snake on stone slab

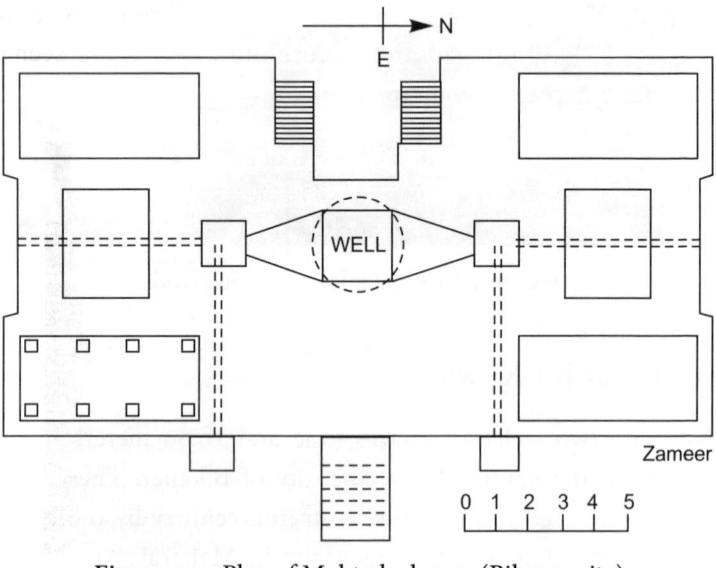

Figure 4.19 Plan of Mohto ka kuwa, (Bikaner city)

Regaron Ka Kuwa

This is located about 200 metres north of the Shivbari talab. It is an old well which was probably constructed by an anonymous builder of *Regar* (leather worker) caste. The family members operate a tube-well on the well, to draw water to irrigate a plot of 14 *bighas* to raise vegetables. This means that the structure was originally constructed by the members of this menial caste. Now it is maintained by Ramchand since 1940 and its photographs show the well, which is in working condition[52] (see Figure 4.20).

Figure 4.20 Vegetables producing land

Acharyon Ka Kuwa

There are two wells 20 metres long and 10.60 meters broad, located on the south-west of the city of Bikaner. These wells were constructed in the late seventeenth century by the family members of Acharya Pushkarna Brahmin. Maharaja Anup Singh granted 1200 *bighas* of land to a Brahmin namely Dharni Dhar

Acharji to excavate two wells for irrigating the surrounding land. Later on, the granter dug out two wells and started to cultivate adjoined area[53]. The wells are located just about 360 fts away in the slope of Harsolao tank.

These two wells were receiving water from the underground current emanating from the adjacent Harsolao tank. Local people call it an underground *nadi* i.e., river. The water percolates from the tank, runs in the form of a stream and gets tapped in a well dug for this purpose (see Figure 4.21 & 4.22).

Interestingly, these *charas*-operated wells were constructed exclusively for irrigation. At this point of time it is difficult to say what was being raised in the former period but now all kinds of vegetables are grown by a gardener family on contract[54].

Two separate inscriptions (VS 1751/AD 1694) are extant and put in the front of each well. In addition, two *parwanas* of VS 1741/AD 1684 and VS 1776/AD 1719 are in the possession of the owners.

Figure 4.21 Acharyon ka kuwa (Bikaner city)

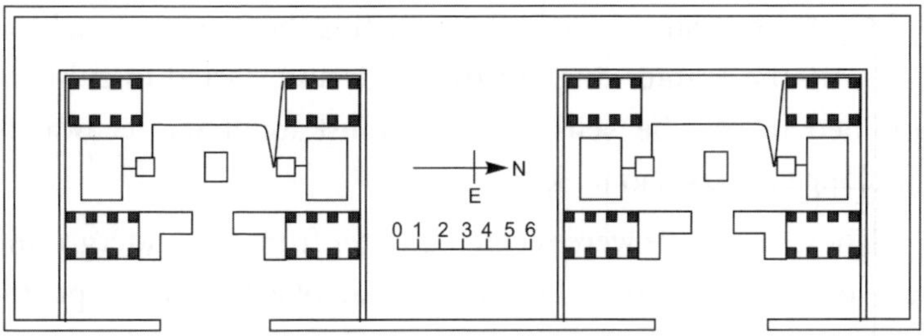

Figure 4.22 Ground plan of Acharyon ka kuwa

The erection of this enormous tank had raised the level of ground-water of the surroundings tract. This is confirmed by the existence of two wells, just few metres away from the tanks. These two wells always remained full of water because of the Harsolao tank[55]. It is interesting to note that the main source of water of these two wells was the Harsolao talab situated around 200 metres away. When water level of the *talab* too raised after rains obviously the level of the *talab* raised and due to percolation the level of these two wells also raised (see Figure 4.23 (a) & 4.23 (b).

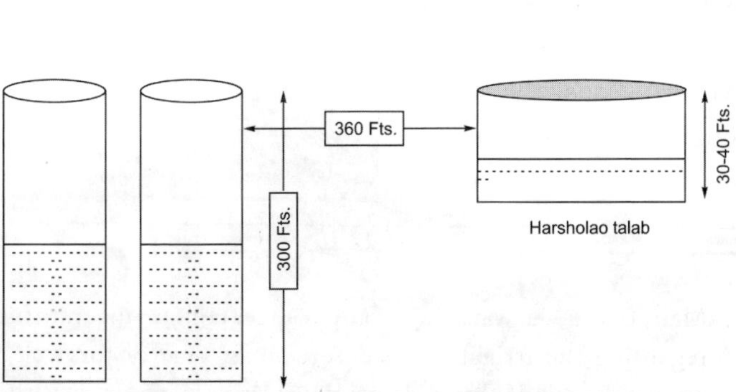

Figure 4.23 (a) Water level of Acharyon ka kuwa and Harsolao talab before the rains

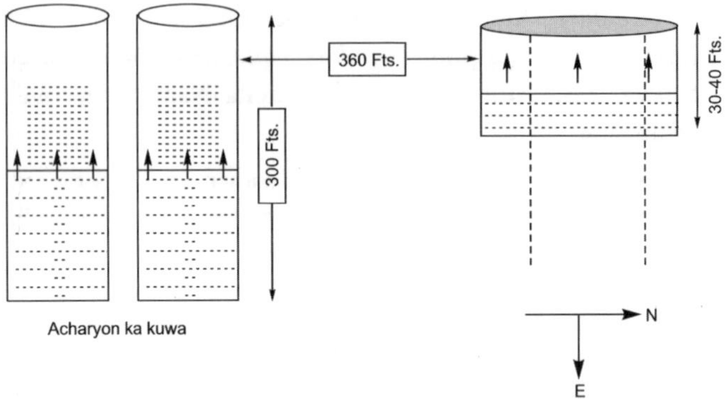

Figure 4.23 (b) Water level of Acharyon ka kuwa and Harsolao talab after the rains

The planners of the wells seem to have the knowledge about the science of underground water movement. Since the water-bodies were located on the slope of the tank, therefore, water percolated in the ground would have made an underground passage known in local parlance as *gupt nadi* which used to pass through the wells and thus raised its water level. It was an exceptional technique to store each drop of rain-water and harvest it. Thus, the water level of the wells could be raised through percolation.

NOTES

1. Many of the Marwari/Rajasthani sources contain the information regarding the irrigation in desert areas. One of the well-liked among these is Muhnot Nainsi, *Marwar-ra-pargana-ri-Vigat*, ed., Narain Singh Bhati, Vol-II, Jodhpur Rajasthan Prachya Vidya Pratishthan, Jodhpur, 1969. Modern work such as; B.L.Bhadani. *'Peasants, Artisan and Entrepreneur Economy of Marwar in the*

17th Century', Rawat Publication, Jaipur, 1999; *Dying Wisdom, Rise, Fall and Potential of India's Traditional Water Harvesting System*, eds., Anil Agarwal and Sunita Narain, reprint, CSE, Delhi, 2005.

2. *Rajasthan District Gazetteers*, Bikaner, ed., K.K. Sehgal, Government of Rajasthan, Jaipur, 1972, p.1.
3. Ibid., p. 411.
4. Ibid.
5. G.H. Ojha, *Bikaner Rajya Ka Itihas*, pt.-I, First Edition, Ajmer, 1939, p. 42. *Rajasthan District Gazetteers*, Bikaner, op. cit., p.411.
6. Ibid., p. 3.
7. Ibid.
8. *Dying Wisdom, Rise, Fall and Potential of India's Traditional Water Harvesting System*, op. cit., pp.104-05. [The eastern part of Jodhpur district was full of wells and also more fertile. Both spring and autumn crops were being raised. A variety of water-lifts were used to draw water from wells].
9. Ibid. p.105. [Gajner, a lake is located at a distance of 32 km from Bikaner city. It is about 0.4 km long and 183 /273 mts across. The water of this lake mostly was being utilized for drinking and bathing purposes, but in the years of good rainfall wheat and mustard were also grown in the lands of the neighbouring areas. It gave great relief to the weary travellers passing through the dreary desert, and was beneficial to the citizens of Bikaner who oppressed by intense summer heat, had to take resort to its bank for picnic and pleasure. See, *Rajasthan District Gazetteers*, Bikaner, op. cit., p.3].
10. G.H. Ojha, *Bikaner Rajya Ka Itihas*, pt.-I, First Edition, op. cit., p. 10. [According to him, generally the depth of well was more than 300 fts while Doctor Moor, got water into 400 fts deep at a village called Natava. At some places its depth was 20 fts].
11. An inscription is available on the slab near the *talab*.
12. Braj Ratan Joshi, *Jal Aur Samaj*, Pushtak Sansar, Jaipur, 2005, p.13.

13. 'Bikaner Ke Talab' ed., Hem Sharma in *Rajasthan Patrika* in 1993. (As quoted by Braj Ratan Joshi, op., cit., p. 13. [Generally *talab* contains many *ghats* such as *janana ghat, mardana ghat, gau ghat, khaki ghat, panyar ghat, dang ghat, kriya ghat, and syahu ghat,* etc. while in *talais* mainly contain; *panyar ghat, gau ghat and mardana ghat*, due to small size of the area of the *talais,* for details see Braj Ratan Joshi, op. cit., pp.48-49].
14. Braj Ratan Joshi, op. cit., p. 13. [Physical survey and many interviews of the sites have been conducted and they have recorded informations from the locals that many of the small *talabs* and *talais* have been destroyed by the persons who needed new constructions near it, which means the process of urbanization directly or indirectly affected these water-bodies].
15. P. W. Powlett *(official political agency*, Alwar, 1874), *Gazetteer of the Bikaner State,* reprint, Government Press, Bikaner, 1932.
16. *Bikaner Ghazal*, written by Udaychand Matheran in VS 1763 AD 1706.
17. *Dying Wisdom, Rise, Fall and Potential of India's Traditional Water Harvesting System*, op. cit., p.105; G.H.Ojha, *Bikaner Rajya Ka Itihas*, op. cit., pp. 6-7.
18. Ibid., p.105.
19. The Ranisar Lake of Jodhpur, situated aside the Mehrangarh fort was reserved for the use of the nobility and was being pulled inside the fort; but the water of the adjacent Padmasar Lake was being used by local populace. The Balsamand Lake in Jodhpur made by the Rajas, was also reserved for specific purpose and people were not allowed to use it even for drinking.
20. *Dying Wisdom, Rise, Fall and Potential of India's Traditional Water Harvesting System*, op. cit., p.106.
21. Ibid.
22. Ibid.
23. Ibid.
24. Ibid.
25. Ibid.

26. The region of *mudiya kankar* known for its excellent run off characteristics.
27. Ibid.
28. Ibid.
29. Ibid.
30. Physical survey of the site.
31. Physical survey and interviews of the site. Dr. Rajendra Kumar assisted author to survey this site.
32. G.H.Ojha, *Bikaner Rajya Ka Itihas*, op. cit., p. 48.
33. Physical survey and interviews of the site.
34. G.H.Ojha, *Bikaner Rajya Ka Itihas*, op. cit., p. 48.
35. Chandramani Singh, ed., *Protected Monuments of Rajasthan*, First Edition, Jawahar Kala Kendra, Jaipur, 2002, pp.128-129. In our survey, we explored atleast two *beris* exist in the beds of *talabs*. Braj Ratan Joshi has given this number seven, but five of them might have lost their existence. He also mentioned that *beris* were available only in two *talabs* in Bikaner city; one *beri* in Devikund sagar and seven in Kalyan sagar. See Braj Ratan Joshi, op. cit., pp. 25 and 46.
36. Ibid.
37. Ibid.
38. G.H.Ojha, *Bikaner Rajya Ka Itihas*, op. cit., p. 48.
39. Physical survey and interviews of the site.
40. Ibid.
41. Ibid.
42. Ibid.
43. Interviews of the old men and the saints residing in the temple. Also see, Braj Ratan Joshi, op. cit., p. 16.
44. Physical survey and interviews of the site.
45. Ibid.
46. *Lekha and jama kharach bahi* of VS 1745-48/AD 1688-91 (s.no.20 *bahi* no.55), Rajasthan States Archives, Bikaner.

47. Physical survey and interviews of the site.
48. Ibid.
49. Ibid.
50. Ibid.
51. Ibid.
52. Interviews of the *Regur* family; this well is still in operation and its water is used to grow vegetables.
53. Details are available in *Shri Ram ka basta* and *Bikaner bahiyat*, Rajasthan State Archives, Bikaner.
54. Ibid., Survey and interview with the owner of the site (land). Wells were important to irrigate the field to produce vegetables.

    [According to A.J. Qaisar, the simplest technique was to draw water with a rope and bucket by hands without any mechanical aid. He said that obviously, the bucket was small in size and this operation could not provide adequate water for large fields. He further said that infact none of the paintings clearly show the use of this method for irrigation. It was used to draw water for domestic use. But he does not deny the use of rope-bucket technique for irrigating small fields to grow crops. Probably most of these vegetables did not require much water. For more details see A.J. Qaisar, 'Agricultural Technology in Mughal Paintings' in *Medieval India 3 Researches in the History of India* ed., B.L.Bhadani, Manohar, 2012, pp.83-84. Author here comments that this technique was most probably used in medieval period in the area where water table was not very deep whereas in Rajasthan, particularly in desert areas, this hand-pulling water technique (rope-bucket) was not possible because depth of the wells were more than 300 fts. A.J. Qaisar further explains about the method in which the employment of the pulleys combined with the rope-bucket contraption was once again activated manually. Pulleys needed lesser amount of human energy and therefore, comparatively larger bags or buckets could be used. But in his another explanation he said that an improved variety of the rope-bucket pulley contraption was to employ a pair of oxen to replace manpower. This method was used specifically

for irrigation purposes and was called the *charas*-operated technique. See A.J. Qaisar, 'Agricultural Technology in Mughal Paintings' op. cit., pp.83-84. Author of the book agreed that the last method was useful in desert regions.This method was also adopted by the desert people to pull water for irrigation, for example, Acharyon ka kuwan, Bikaner city, Rajasthan].

55. B.L. Bhadani and Jibraeil, say the same thing in their work on 'Water Harvesting and Techniques of Irrigation in Urban Areas during Medieval Period: A Case Study of Bikaner', published in a seminar proceedings *Urbanization and Trade Routes of Rajasthan*, ed., S.P. Vyas, Jodhpur, 2011, pp. 64-77.

■■■

5

Water Harvesting Techniques in Churu, Chhapar and Bidasar

The region of Churu mostly faced scarcity of water. Here rains generally fall once in two or three years. Under these circumstances the people of the Thar Desert were always thirsty for water. Therefore, they developed techniques to store water for more than one year for their consumption. They had *kund* or *kundis* in their houses and constructed *beris* in the beds of the *talab*. They had developed technique to harvest water for drinking and other purposes. An attempt has been made in this chapter to study the technique which was adopted for harvesting water by the locals in desert's urban areas like Churu, Chhapar and Bidasar.

Qasbas Churu, Chhapar and Bidasar were surveyed during our visits (see Figure 5.1). The survey revealed the revenue records of the *qasba* Churu during the 18th and 19th centuries. The information thus collected from the records as well as through the field surveys is discussed briefly in this present chapter.

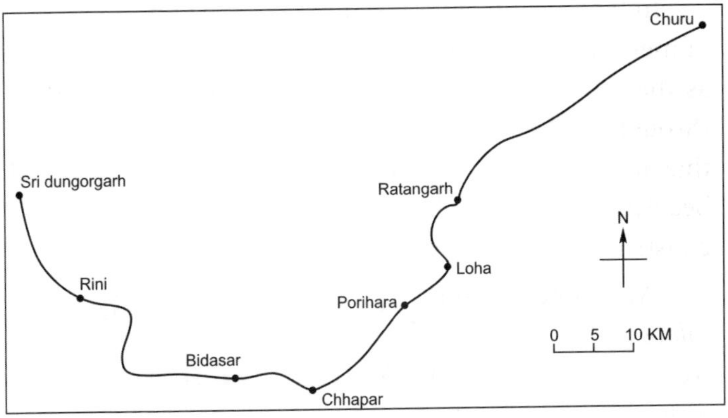

Figure 5.1 Map of surveyed areas

QASBA CHURU

Churu a town of historic importance is said to have been founded by a Jat named Chuhru in AD 1620, thus it was named after him[1]. It lies in 28°18′ latitude north and 74°58′ longitude east and is the headquarters of the district of the same name[2]. This town is surrounded by the sand-dunes of the Thar Desert[3] and is known as the "gate of the desert"[4]. Churu is the home of many wealthy persons having business connections all over India[5] and during the 18th century it emerged as the biggest trading centre of Rajasthan[6]. A good number of *sarais/ dharmshalas* are found here which fulfilled the requirements of the traders, especially during the 18th century[7] (see Appendix 5.1). It is surrounded by sand-dunes[8], and bounded in the north by Ganganagar district, in the east by Sikar and Jhunjhunu districts of Rajasthan and Hisar district of Haryana, in the south by the district of Nagaur and in the west by Bikaner district[9]. Churu has been one of the important towns in the 18th century Rajasthan, specifically in the Rathor principality of the Bikaner state[10].

In the town, there was not much scope for the development of methods of irrigation[11]. The canal irrigation was not possible as there is no perennial or semi-perennial river flowing in or through the boundaries of the district[12]. It is interesting to note that in our survey we have recorded more than five big and beautiful *talabs* and also more than 80 wells, which have been constructed almost with same features of architecture[13].

We did not get much information about irrigation by these *talabs* and wells. But it became clear from our survey that every well and *talab* had at least a garden (called *bagichi*) where the water of the wells was being used for irrigating the *bagichis* to produce vegetables. And near these *talabs* and wells, we also found haveli/*sarais*/temples, which used this water for domestic purposes. Most of the water-bodies appear to have been located on the trade route passing through the city. Here, we are providing photographs and plans of these water-bodies[14].

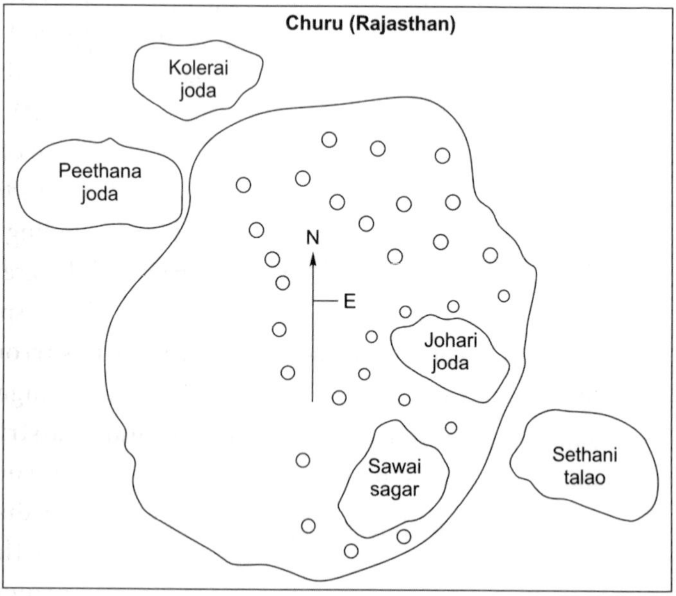

Figure 5.2 Plotted water bodies of *qasba* Churu

A large number of water-bodies demonstrate the level of consciousness of the local people about water conservation and therefore they had developed well-knit water-harvesting structures in the heart of the desert. This shows the capacities and capabilities of the local people to fight against the scarcities of the nature. Their efforts had converted the desert into an oasis and changed the environment of the area. Even today we can see a large number of small gardens and equally a large number of trees[15].

TALAB/JODA

Sethani ka Joda (*Johad*)

- It is a beautiful *joda/talab* of Churu town which is located at a distance of 4 miles in the west of *qasba* Churu[16] (see Figure 5.3). It was constructed by a well-known lady, Janaki Devi Bagala (wife of Bhagwandas ji Bagala), popularly known as *Sethani* (About *Johad* or *Joda*, see Glossary of this book).
- This *talab* is still in use.
- The main catchment area is from the city side. While inlets in the form of holes are available on all sides of the *talab*.
- A well is situated near the *talab* in the east at a distance of 200 metres.
- *Gau ghat* (for animals) is constructed in the north of the *talab*.
- It is more than 40 feet deep.

Figure 5.3 Sethani joda (*talab*)

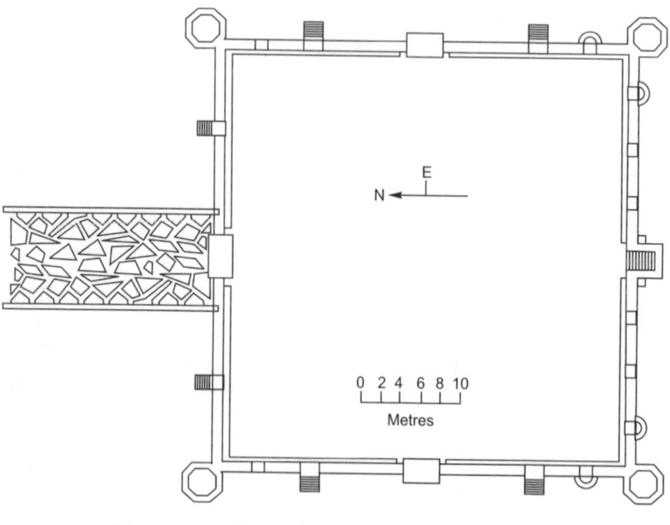

Figure 5.4 Plan of Sethani ka joda, Churu

Johari Sagar Joda

This *talab* is also known as Dakida Joda. It has been renovated by a resourceful person of *qasba* Churu in 2009 (see Figure 5.5 & 5.6).

- Presently it is more than 20 feet deep.
- It was constructed by a *baniya* Joharimal Potdar of Ramgarh to provide drinking water to people.
- A *haveli/sarai* is constructed just in front of the *talab* by Bhagwandas Bagla of Churu. According to a knowledgeable person, this *talab* was constructed to procure drinking water. The *haveli* was constructed for serving those involved in trading and passing through this place. This means the *haveli* was functioning as a *sarai*[17].

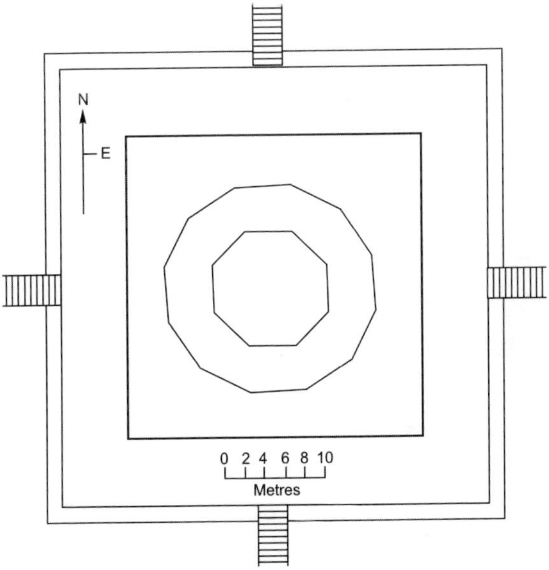

Figure 5.5 Plan of Johri sagar joda (*talab*), Churu

- Approximately five wells, three *bagichis* and three *havelis* constructed adjacent to Johari talab, are still alive. Therefore, it can be said that it was one of the halting centres of Churu for the traders passing through the *qasba*[18].

Figure 5.6 Johari sagar joda (*talab*), Churu

Sawai Sagar Joda

- This *joda* (*talab*) was constructed by a *baniya* Ganesh Das Khemaka[19].
- This *Joda* is situated within the boundary of a garden known as Sawai sagar bagichi which is flourishing as a result of the water of *talab* available here. Nowadays it is also being used to grow vegetables in the garden[20] (see Figure 5.7).
- The garden is spread over 10 *bighas*.

Figure 5.7 Sawai sagar joda (*talab*), Churu

Peethana Joda

- It is situated on the slope side towards the west of the *qasba*.
- Near this *talab* we have traced two wells but none is in use.
- Adjacent to the *talab*, a *sarai* is constructed while a temple stands opposite to it (see Figure 5.8 & 5.9).
- We have also found an inscription of VS 1747/AD 1690, which is on a *slab* and is attached to this *talab*[21].

Figure 5.8 Peethana joda (*talab*)

Figure 5.9 Cenotaph at a corner of Peethana joda (*talab*)

Kalara Joda

- It is situated on the Churu -Taranagar road at a distance of 7 kms towards west of the *qasba*[22].
- It is also like Peethana Joda; but it is not possible to measure it, as it is surrounded by wild grass.

The excavation of a large number of tanks and taping rain-water in them proved beneficial in raising the water table of the area near to the surface which made digging of wells possible. This is the reason why a large number of wells existed in and around the *qasba*.

WELLS

We have explored more than 80 wells, and some of them are more than 400 years old. Most of them have been constructed on the same pattern and are almost 200-300 years old. One interesting fact came to light that many of them are located near some *baari/bagichi* (small gardens). These small gardens were being watered by these wells. According to knowledgeable persons the Dhanuka kuwa was constructed to procure water for drinking as well as irrigating purposes[23]. Presently, we can find two big *baaris* producing vegetables there. It is surprising that in the "heart of desert", the *baniyas* constructed numerous wells not only to solve the problem of drinking water but to water a large numbers of *bagichis* too. For the sample study we have taken photographs of more than 50 wells and measured more than 10 wells. A few of them are as follows:

Bhagwandas Ka Kuwa

It was constructed by Bhagwandas Bagla, a *baniya* of Churu. Water of this well was not available for drinking purposes as it had a saltish taste. Therefore, it was merely used for irrigating

the *bagichis*. Presently, it is under the possession of Mangilal (65 yrs old man) who purchased this, a fully *charas*-operated well. This well is more than 200 feet deep and is situated near Sethani *talab*[24] (see Figure 5.10).

Figure 5.10 Bhagwandas ka kuwa (Wooden made wheel (pulley) for pulling the water bucket)

Shakar Kuwa

It was constructed by Anwanmal Potdar, brother of Joharimal Potdar, a *baniya* of Ramgarh (Shekhawati) [25]. It is situated in the north of the Johari Sagar talab, just 20 metres away. It contains sweet water; therefore, it is called Shakar kuwa. According to knowledgeable persons and even by the owner of the well, its water was consumed not only for drinking purposes but also for raising vegetables in the *baari* (*bagichi*) [26]. According to the owner Puranmal, a 50 years old mali, "We were producing carrot, cabbage, raddish and other vegetables till a few years ago". It is also said that near Johari talab and Shakar kuwa, many *bagichis*, *dharmasalas* (*sarais*), *havelis* were constructed for the traders and *karavans* to stay here and take rest for a few days, if needed [27]. This phenomenon shows the importance of the *qasba*.

Baninathji Ka Kuwa

This is still in operation. Approximately 2 *bighas* of land is being irrigated to produce vegetables for the local market of the *qasba*[28] (see Figure 5.11(a) & (b).

Figure 5.11 (a) Baninathji ka kuwa

Figure 5.11 (b) Cultivating land

Lohiya Ki Kuin

This well (*kuin*[29]) was constructed by a *baniya* business family. According to the locals the water of this well was previously sweet but later on it became saltish.

Jatiji Ka Kuwa

It was an unoperated well which had very strong base made of bricks. Locals informed us that water of this well was being used for irrigation of the small *bagichi* attached to it.

Mantriyon Ka Kuwa

It is a beautiful well constructed by the trading community and situated inside the city. According to the people residing there, the traders used to halt near it to use its water. It is a fact that in 18th and early 19th centuries, this town was known for its trading activities (see Figure 5.12).

Figure 5.12 Mantriyon ka kuwa

Maniharon Ka Kuwa

This well was constructed by Manihar community previously for their own use but later on it was also used freely by other communities of the town as well (see Figure 5.13).

Figure 5.13 Maniharon ka kuwa

Besides the wells having dicussed above, the other wells explored by our survey team are: Khemaka kuwa, Sawai sagar kuwa, Goyanka kuwa, Dhanuka kuwa, Chamaron ka kuwa, Ram sagar kuwa, Din sagar kuwa, Bagla ka kuwa, Gaddha sagar kuwa, Bahausi ka kuwa, Ram Gopal Joharmal Khemaka kuwa, Gogaji ke mandir ka kuwa, Masjid ki kuin, Lila ka kuwa, Bahad ka kuwa, Kanhaiya Lalji Bagla ka kuwa, Pediwal ka kuwa, Gausa ka kuwa, Naathji ka kuwa, Natthuji Gosain ka kuwa, Mudda ka kuwa, Cholava kuwa, Shahar ka kuwa, Champa bagh kuwa, Madan Niwas bagh kuwa, Balika Mahavidyalaya ka kuwa, Mishron ka kuwa, Potdaron ka kuwa, Seksariya kuwa, etc.

QASBA CHHAPAR

It is a small *qasba* in the Churu district and is located at a distance of 95 kms to the south-west of the city. In our survey we found many tanks located in a row, such as Bada talab, Chetlai, Nathlai, Akolai and Fauzi talai (see Figure 5.14). All these water-bodies are located from west to east, forms a depression since the land their slope is from south to north. Therefore, main source of water is located in the south of the *qasba*. We also traced two wells (one has lost its existence and another with its extant structure is saltish). Therefore, people of the *qasba* depend on *beris* (which are located in the bed area of *talabs*) for drinking water. According to the locals, these *talabs* are being used for drinking as well as irrigation purposes. Their details (photographs and plans) are as follows:

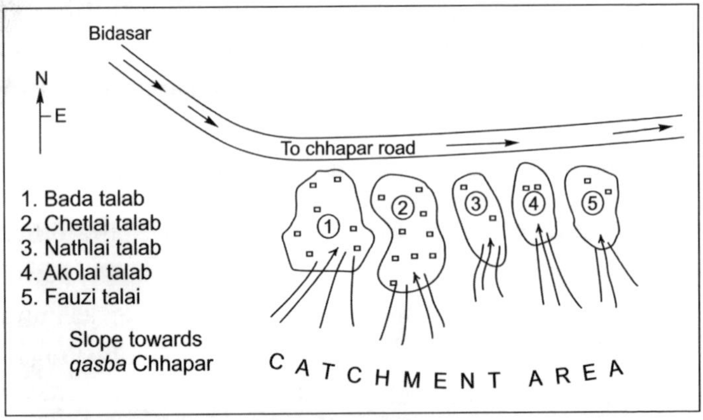

Figure 5.14 Technique of irrigation in the desert area of *qasba* Chhapar (not on scale)

Bada Talab

This is the Bada talab which has fully dried up, but in its bed a number of *beris* are constructed and people of the area use them for collecting drinking water (see Figure 5.15).

Figure 5.15 Showing *beris* on the bed of Bada talab (Chhapar)

Chetlai Talab

This talab was constructed by a Jat farmer to procure drinking water as well as water for irrigation. It is circular in shape and has a metalled (*pucca*) tank connected to Bada talab. The overflow of the Bada talab falls into Chetlai talab (see Figure 5.16).

Figure 5.16 Circular talab of Chetlai (Chhapar)

Nathlai Talab

It is a very big *talab* and has many *beris* in its bed. According to elders of this *qasba*, the overflow of the Chetlai talab falls into Nathlai talab (see Figure 5.17).

Figure 5.17 *Beries* in Nathlai (Chhapar)

Akolai Talab

It is a small *talai* and has very little depth. Therefore, generally this *talab* has less water than the other. It is connected with Nathlai talab on one side and Fauzi on the other.

Fauzi Talai

This is a big and beautiful *kachcha talai*, which has many *beris* in its bed. It contains water mostly because of it is located in a depression and is connected with other *talabs*. The overflow of other tanks falls into this tank (see Figure 5.18).

Figure 5.18 *Beries* of Fauzi talai (Chhapar)

QASBA BIDASAR

It is also a small *qasba* and located at a distance of 25 kms in the north-west of the *qasba* Chhapar and claims its own historical importance. It was established by the younger brother of Rao Bika. It is as old as Bikaner. We have surveyed this *qasba* and traced a beautiful *talab*, and more than four *joda* and numerous wells. Some of them are more than 400 years old. Their details are as follows:

Manaksar Talab

It is a good looking *talab* situated on the Dungargarh-Chhapar route. We surveyed two *sarais* situated at the two corners of the *talab,* which shows that the *qasba* was located on a trade junction. In the east of this *talab* at a distance of around 100 feet a well is also located. The tank has vast catchment area on its three sides (see Figure 5.19 & 5.20).

Figure 5.19 Manaksar talab (Bidasar)

Figure 5.20 Two *sarais* very close to Manaksar talab

WELLS

There are more than seven wells in the *qasba*. Of these the oldest one was constructed at the time of the settlement of the *qasba*, that is, in the last decade of the 15th century; while new wells

are merely 150 years old. Sand stone, another important rock of this area is found in some wells. It is actually quarried about 1.6 km (1 mile) west where it crops up[30]. The details about wells are mentioned below:

Tilok Sagar Kuwa

The nomenclature of the tank shows that the sub-soil water is available in abundance here. It is still in use with the help of a tube-well.

Pratap Sagar Kuwa

Similarly, this well too has enormous underground water and presently it has been closed due to some construction in the area.

Beri Kuwa

It is an old *kuwa* and has been ruined.

Chautina Kuwa

It is the oldest *kuwa* and has been ruined.

Nemichand Nahata Kuwa

It was constructed by a Jain called Nemichand, and is not in use.

Thanmal Kuwa

It is also closed.

Chiman Khad Kuwa

It is not in use.

The existence of a large number of wells show the availability of sub-soil water in abundance in the area. This became possible because of the excavation of tanks in large numbers whose percolated water made it possible to locate. It is also important to note that in the 18th century this *qasba* was known as a trade centre. Traders frequently visited and stayed here because of the adequate availability of water, besides other facilities.

NOTES

1. *Rajasthan District Gazetteers*, Churu, ed., K.K. Sehgal, Government of Rajasthan, Jaipur, 1970, pp. 336-337.
2. Ibid.
3. Ibid. [The sand-dunes ranging in height from 6 mts to 30 mts (about 20 feets to 100 feets), suggest the ribbed appearance of a sea-shore].
4. Anil Agarwal and Sunita Narain, eds., *Dying Wisdom, Rise, Fall and Potential of India's Traditional Water Harvesting System*, reprint, CSE, Delhi, 2005; *Rajasthan District Gazetteers*, Churu, op. cit., p.1.
5. Physical survey of the sites.
6. Govind Agarwal, *Churu Mandal Ka Shodhpurna-Itihas,* Lok Sanskriti Sodh Sansthan, Churu, 1974. Also see Jibraeil, 'Churu: A city of the Desert', in a Journal *Shodh Patrika* Year 53, *Ank* 1-4, Institute of Rajasthan Studies, Udaipur, January-December 2002, pp.72-82. Cf. *Sava bahis* of different years which are available in the Rajasthan State Archives, Bikaner.
7. Physical survey of the sites.
8. *Rajasthan District Gazetteers*, Churu, op. cit., p.4.
9. Ibid., p.1.
10. Govind Agrawal, *Churu Mandal Ka Shodhpurn Itihas*, op. cit., p.1.
11. Anil Agarwal and Sunita Narain, eds., *Dying Wisdom, Rise, Fall and Potential of India's Traditional Water Harvesting System*, op. cit.

12. Ibid.
13. Physical survey of the sites.
14. Ibid.
15. Ibid.
16. *Rajasthan District Gazetteers*, Churu, op. cit., p. 337.
17. Interviews done during our physical survey of the sites.
18. Ibid.
19. Ibid.
20. Physical survey of the sites.
21. Ibid.
22. Ibid.
23. Interviews done during our physical survey of the sites.
24. Ibid., [Personally we met the owner of the land].
25. Interviews done during our physical survey of the sites.
26. Ibid., [Personally we met the owner of the land].
27. Interviews taken during our physical survey of the sites.
28. Physical survey of the sites.
29. This kind of water structures are generally found in the deserts of Rajasthan; these are 10-12 mts deep pits dug near tanks to collect the seepage. *Kuis* can also be used to harvest rain-water in areas with meagre rainfall. The mouth of the pit is usually made very narrow. This prevents the collected water from evaporating. The pit gets wider as it holes under the ground, so that water can seep into a large surface area. The openings of these entirely *kuchcha* (earthen) structures are generally covered with planks of wood, or put under lock and key. The water is used sparingly, as a last resource in crisis situations. There is an interesting example that a farmer Magga Ram Suthar of village Pithla in Jaisalmer district in Rajasthan is an engineer skilled in making *kuis/beris*.
30. *Rajasthan District Gazetteers*, Churu, op. cit., p. 7.

6

Water Harvesting and Irrigation Techniques in Jaisalmer

Jaisalmer was founded by king Jaisa or Rao Jaisal, atop a hill, probably bordering a lake called Kanpur Desar, in VS 1212/ AD 1155 [1]; though tradition tells us that there was a well (*kohar*) and a *kund*.[2] The word Jaisalmer is derived from a combination of two words, Jaisal and *meru* (Jaisal's fort) [3]. Jaisalmer got its name not only from its founder, Rao Jasel, but also from the word *mer,* which in local parlance means a rocky area[4]. Thus, apart from its location on a ridge, it has an exceptional status as a rocky oasis in an otherwise boundless sea of aridity that rendered Jaisalmer a measure of invincibility down the ages[5]. During Akbar's reign it got the status of *pargana.* At the time of the compilation of *Ain-i-Akbari* of Abul Fazl, it was a part of the *sarkar* of Bikaner.[6] Later during the time of Shahjahan, Jaisalmer acquired a separate status of *sarkar* with *jamadami* (estimated revenue) of 76,10,000 *dams.*[7] Jaisalmer is a symbolic state regarding the water structures in the town and its villages.

Jaisalmer, headquarter of the district and once the capital of a princely state, is located on 26°55′ north latitude and 70°55′

east longitude[8]. The town is situated at the southern end of a low range of hills and is surrounded by a stone wall, about five kms in circuit, three to five metres high, two to three metres thick and strengthened by bastions and corner towers[9]. Within this wall, towards the south, there is the fort[10]. The Jaisalmer fort is the second oldest fort of Rajasthan[11]. The fort is built on a hillock 75 metres above the surrounding country, founded by Rawal Jaisal[12]. Inside the fort, there were atleast three sweet water wells and in the town below another six wells[13]. It is noticeable that Jaisalmer has a large number of water structures and monuments, attracting the historians and tourists towards it (see Appendix 6.1). The fort is approachable through four successive gates known as the Akhai Pole, Ganesh Pole, Buta Pole and Hawa Pole[14]. The palaces of the ruler built atop the main entrance form an imposing pile crowned by a huge umbrella of metal, mounted on a stone shaft, a solid symbol of dignity of which the Bhati chiefs were justly proud. But the interior is ill-arranged and the space is frittered away in numerous small appartments[15]. Within the fort four Vaishnava and eight Jaina temples exist. It is believed that the oldest temple was built around AD 1332 by Jai Singh Cholasah and dedicated to Parshvanath[16]. The most attractive structure of the town is the Ghadisar tank, which was built by Rawal Gharsi (Ghatsi) in AD 1367[17] (see Figure 6.1 & 6.2). Water was obtained from this tank, located at a short distance south-east of the gate of the same name[18]. According to one of the records, this tank was the chief source of water supply to Jaisalmer town until 1965[19]. Its water lasted throughout the year. The reservoir along with its main gateway is the pride of Jaisalmer and many poems have been composed in its praise. Today, its catchment area has been destroyed; therefore, water level of the tank has gone very low. Even fish are becoming extinct due to less amount of water in the tank.

Figure 6.1 A cenotaph in the centre of Ghadisar talab, Jaisalmer

Figure 6.2 Tilon ki pol monument (main gateway) on the banks of Ghadisar talab, Jaisalmer

Following line of a *Ghazal* composed by Mehta Umed Singh shows people's love for Ghadisar Lake, Jaisalmer city, Jaisalmer.

(As quoted by Chandramani Singh in his monumental edited book *Protected Monuments of Rajasthan* - p.246.)

Takht Jesan Tako Jaanat Hai Jahaan Tako
Sab Mulkan Mein Naam Atibhari Hai
Killa Hai Bhoorgarh Bhoop Jawahir Singh Adhik
Chhabi Pyari Aur Fauz Dal Apari Hai.
Ryot Marwari Chhata Ghadsisar Ki Bhari
Jahaan Bharat Neer Lakhon Aur Kiror Panihari Hai.
Maheta Kahai Umed Singh Vaho
Jesan Naath Riyasat Tumhari Badshahat Se Niyari Hai.

KHADEEN
(Water Harvesting and Irrigation Technique)

Muhnot Nainsi furnishes information on the geography and location of villages which he mentions while describing the different geographical zones of the region. He especially mentions villages in geographical blocks, namely, *khadal* and *kharad*. The literal meaning of *khadal* appears to be an unleveled land between small hilly areas. The major portion of this area was located between 300 metres high hills. These low lying areas acted as water basins during the rainy season. Land became fertile due to these depressions. The villages, recorded by Nainsi, are found in the north-west of Jaisalmer, while Bankidas records the location of *khadal* in the west[20]. A nucleus of thirty villages was colonized here in this geographical block. The *kharad*, too, is a specific geographical area known as '*kharad-budha-ro*' which means colonized by a person named Budha. The villages of this area are found in the north-east of Jaisalmer. Nainsi fixes its location near

Pokaran and Phalodi[21]; numerous wells and big tanks are also described in this belt. Again, this area of *kharad*, too, was located in the north-east between high ridges, from 300 to 381 metres. Besides, there was a big dry run which had the full capacity to contain large amount of water to be used for irrigation.

The east part of Jaisalmer which appears to be more fertile possessed fifty villages[22]. This area was irrigated by a seasonal river named the river 'Kak'. Secondly, it contained hills and depressions. The village Thaiat contained *unav*[23] (natural depression) and *khadeen*[24] (man-made canals to draw water from the depression). This explains the comparatively larger concentration of villages in this direction. Interestingly, Nainsi's information broadly corresponds with the actual physical geography. The district is situated in the extreme west of Rajasthan and forms the major part of the Great Indian Desert. It is located between 26°-01′ to 28°-02′ north latitudes and 69°-29′ to 72°-20′ east longitudes[25]. The district is bounded on the west, north and north-west by Pakistan and on the north-east by Bikaner; on the south lies Barmer and on the east Jodhpur.[26]

Khadeen was first designed by the Paliwal Brahmins of Jaisalmer, residing in western Rajasthan in the 15th century. According to many scholars who have worked on water-bodies of desert Rajasthan[27], a *khadeen* is also called a *dhora*. It is an ingenious construction designed to harvest surface run off water for agriculture. Its main feature is a very long (100-300 metres) earthen embankment built across the lower hill slopes lying below gravely uplands. Sluices and spillways allow excess water to drain off. The *khadeen* system is based on the principle of harvesting rain-water on farmland and subsequent use of this water-saturated land for crop production. We surveyed both the river Kok/Kak and one famous *khadeen* called *masur khadeen*[28], near the Kuldhara settlement (see Appendix 6.2) of the region

(see Figure 6.4: Ground plan of the *khadeen*). When the water dries up, wheat and gram are grown in the area[29]. Most of the seasonal streams are only *nallahs* with limited catchment areas[30]. The waters are locked by the inhabitants to form *khadeens* used for cultivation[31]. Twenty-two villages that earlier belonged to *pargana* Kotra located in the south, were annexed to Jaisalmer. Nainsi does not offer further geographical information of this part, but the physical map of the area shows numerous hillocks up to the height of 322 to 656 fts, significant for irrigation.

There are hardly any good wells which can be source of irrigation[32]. According to Erskine, the water in the wells was brakish. The average depth of the wells was 76 metres or 250 fts and one measured by an officer of the Trignometrical Survey of India had a depth of 149 metres or 490 fts[33]. Sometimes sweet water would be struck but it was rare. Besides the wells, *johads*[34] (ponds) are another source of water supply during the rainy season. The accumulated water was used by all the inhabitants, animals as well as human. When there was a good rainfall the ponds would fill up and the water would last till the end of winter; but in deficient years, which were more common, the water would dry within a short time. Then there was not even enough water to drink. If a village was not able to have at least one or two sweet water well, the drinking water had to be brought over covering long distances. Obtaining sufficient quantities of drinking water has been an acute problem for years[35]. A large number of scholars, thinkers have accepted that the people of Jaisalmer were depending on rain-water for the whole year, for drinking as well as irrigation purposes. People had metalled (*pucca*) houses with *tanka* or *kundi* (*hauz*) to store water for at least one year sometimes for even two years for drinking purposes[36]. During the reign of Maharava Jawahar Singh, agriculture flourished. As mostly Jaisalmer had rains once

in two years people would repair their water tanks and construct small *bundha* (bridge) to store the rain-water. They also connect water tanks with one another to store every drop of water in urban and rural areas of Jaisalmer[37].

Nainsi informs us about the *khadeens* of Muhar. The village Muhar is located in the hills of the western part of Jaisalmer and contains 15 villages. The existence of *khadeens* in this area puts this locality in the high fertility zone[38]. In addition, 12 more villages are recorded in this locality. The same numbers of *sansan* villages are also there, probably all over the *pargana*[39]. This gives us a total of 39 villages in the *pargana* of Jaisalmer. Whatever information we have on the above, shows the settlement pattern in the Thar Desert.

Khadeen, though an ancient creation, it was a sound scientific practice during the medieval period carried out by the people of Rajasthan, particularly Jaisalmer. No account of skillful harvesting of rain-water in western Rajasthan can possibly be complete without referring to *khadeen.* Agricultural scientists of arid zone believe that it carries a great importance even in present time[40] for the *Thar* agriculture and land-use. (see Figure 6.3 , 6.4 & 6.5).

Figure 6.3 Masoori gaon (*khadeen*), Jaisalmer

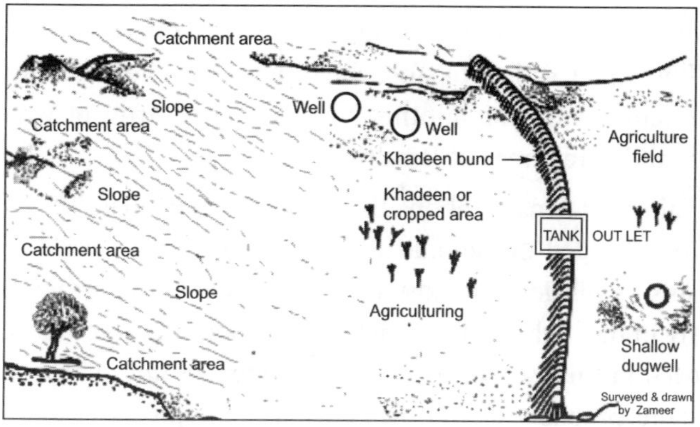

Figure 6.4 Ground plan of masoori khadeen, Jaisalmer

Figure 6.5 Agricultural lands with the use of *khadeen* technique, masoori gaon, Jaisalmer

According to the local behief *khadeen* or *dhora* were planned by the Paliwal Brahmins of Jaisalmer around the 15th century[41]. The immediate rulers would give lands to the Paliwals and ask them to develop *khadeens* on their land. The ownership of the land would remain with the king. Of the grain that was harvested from *khadeen* land, one-fourth (1/4th) would have

to be given to the king. Thus, the Paliwals developed a whole network of *khadeens* in Jaisalmer. According to a source and verified by our survey team, there are still as many as 500 big and small *khadeens* covering an area of 12,140 hectare (around 30,000 acres)[42]. *Khadeens* are also found in the adjoining district of Jodhpur, Barmer and Bikaner[43].

Artificial irrigation forms the backbone of any agrarian society, especially in the absence of perennial rivers or water channels. This assumes a greater significance in the Thar Desert of Jaisalmer where average rainfall was rather very low. Therefore, the utilization of scanty water demands peasant's skills. This consciousness appears to have necessitated the innovation of irrigation techniques suitable for the desert.

Irrigation in the desert was possible only in hard soil and rocky areas[44]. Generally, natural depressions (*undal*) got created between two ridges[45]. Sometimes such depressions had no outlet at all, and hence they formed a kind of lake those in the hills of Kotra and Chohtan. Obviously, this kind of depression would be quite deep and water collected there sometimes would be 100 to 150 fits deep.[46] The circumference of this particular depression lake comes to 3 *kos* (about eight miles).[47] Here, in this lake, when water scales down, it was drained away by lifting water from channels (*beri*) to the surrounding villages. The *beri* has numerous meanings, such as some times it is called channels, other times it may be referred to as a shallow well[48].

Similar kind of depression (*unav*) is created in the west of Jaisalmer. This is known as "*muhar-re-khareen-ro-unav*", (depression of *khadeen* of the village Muhar) and covers the areas of 5 *kos* (about 13 miles).[49] This water basin is bigger than the former. The peculiarity of this is that here about twenty to twenty-five masonry *kosita*-type[50] wells were constructed, irrigating the adjoining large areas. A fair amount of the rain-

water percolates down to be stored as groundwater in sand and gravel[51] raising the water table for irrigation for longer periods. Thus, the surrounding areas acquire fertility to produce *rabi* crops such as wheat, gram and sugarcane.[52]

Two terms-*unav* and *khadeen* have distinct connotations: they have been recorded separately by Nainsi.[53] The former means an exclusively natural depression, while the latter appears to involve human efforts to create dam, canals (both earthen and masonry) and wells.[54] The motive behind these constructions was to drain the water from these basins to adjacent areas. Large number of *khadeens* might have been made in the 17th century by rich peasants.[55] One may suspect a sharp decline in *khadeen* irrigation since the 19th century.[56] These were the finest examples of dam and canal technology of premodern period in the Thar Desert. The magnitude of investment in waterworks and names/castes of their planners and constructors need investigation.[57]

Wells and tanks were also sometimes used for irrigation. The land of village Shekhsar was watered by a large tank of the same name to produce wheat.[58] This was an artificial masonry tank constructed by Shekha (the colonizer of the village) for irrigation. Several villages with the suffix *sar*[59] refer to pond-attracted village settlements[60]. One may presume that the construction of a tank needs masonry work[61] which required a lot of investment. In turn, they provided revenue to the state or *jagirdars*.

The pastoral sector has for long been a mere adjunct of agriculture. There is a need to have drought immune animal to plough the fields and lift water. Moreover, these animals fulfill other needs by producing milk, wool, etc. The state of Jaisalmer possessed some grazing grounds to breed superior cattle for exports to the agricultural zones, and camels as a means of transport.

Maintenance of pasture ground was necessary both at the state level and the village community. Recording of pasturages was done with the view of assessing revenue of the cultivable land in agricultural zone by the premodern state. Nainsi offers us a list of pasturage grounds (*jor*) in Jaisalmer where different varieties of such grass grow.[62] These are located in the east, south, west, north-west and east-west of the town.[63] Total pasturages come to thirty which amounts to nineteen per cent of the village. In addition, the size of wasteland and jungle might have been quite large. This is true even today.[64] Pasturages recorded by Nainsi are of particularly large in size, producing good quality of grass. The khargo pastural ground is reported to have been quite big. Next in size, located in the south of Jaisalmer, was about 5 miles (two *kos*) in circumference, while that of Nachna was 2½ miles (one *kos*).[65] Location of pastures appear to have remarkably corresponded to the water basins or depressions. We do not know about the number of cattle and other animals. A stray reference conveys the existence of large number of horses, camels, buffaloes and she-goats.[66] Existence of good breed of camels is noticed in the *Ain*.[67]

Available information about agricultural production is quite scanty but very useful. This explodes the general impression or myth about the "scarcity" of crops produced in the desert. For information on crops we are exclusively indebted to Nainsi. In addition to *bajra*, *jowar*, *mung* and other pulses, references are also found to wheat, (*katha* and *sewanj* variety), *chhontra*, gram, cotton, sugarcane, rice (very rare) and other crops.[68] The references about crops totals up more than twelve which is equivalent to those of the Jodhpur state. Moreover, Nainsi records the yield and the total production in one village named Bap.[69] The productivity of this locality is reported to have been sixty times: one maund of wheat-seed would yield sixty times,

that means, the production of sixty maunds of wheat. The total wheat production is estimated to have been five lakh maunds in presumably one *rabi* season.[70] The production of sugarcane shows the availability of water in abundance though in some areas where sufficient water had been stored, i.e., Bara Bagh. Vegetable production was also taken care of. The production of both cotton[71] and sugarcane seems to have declined and ended completely since then. Only this much can be inferred from the meager evidence that we have today that the peasants of Jaisalmer did not lag behind the peasants of other areas.

Table 6.1 Comparison of caste-population between 1643 and 1921

S.No.	Castes	1643	1921 census[72]
1	Oswal	7,500	181
2	Maheswari	2,500	6,015
3	Paliwal Brahmans	2,500	NA
Total		12,500	6,196

NA: Not Available

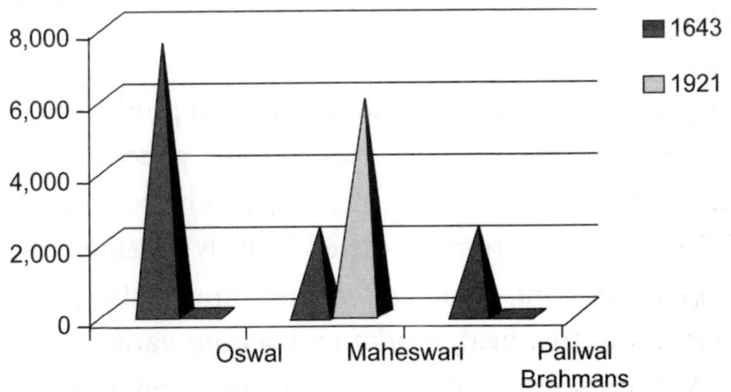

Figure 6.6 This graph is based on the above table titled 'Comparison of caste-population between 1643 and 1921'

From the above table it is clear that the population of the Oswals, Maheswaris and Paliwal Brahmins in 1643 AD was 7500, 2500, and 2500, respectively; whereas the total population was

12500. When we compare these figures with those of the Census 1921, we find that the number got declined from 12500 to 6196, which indicates a sharp decline in the commercial population during three centuries. It points descending trends in trade and commerce and the accompanying deurbanization. (see Appendix 6.3).

Above study is an attempt at interpreting the data available in Nainsi and the survey of the town. In this endeavour, the efforts of peasants to evolve an indigenous dam-technology (*khadeen*) are highlighted particularly in premodern times; this remarkably suited the desert conditions. This technology enabled them to grow maximum number of crops, though some of them needed more water, such as sugarcane, wheat, and rice. Maintenance of large pasturages means prosperity in terms of animals and their products which substantially supplemented the peasant's income. In the survey we realized that the people of the town were able to manage the water in the desert land, for instance, they successfully constructed many water-bodies for drinking and possibly for irrigation purposes in the town and village areas. For irrigation they created a method of *khadeen* in rural as well as other areas, which is quite commendable.

NOTES

1. Muhnot Nainsi, *Khyat*, ed., B.P. Sakariya, II, Jodhpur, 1962, p.6; G. N. Sharma, *Social Life in Medieval Rajasthan*, L.N. Agarwal, Agra, 1968, p. 49; *Rajasthan District Gazetteers,* Jaisalmer, ed., K. K. Sehgal, Government of Rajasthan, Jaipur, 1973, p.1.
2. Muhnot Nainsi, *Khyat*, ed., B.P. Sakariya, II, op. cit., p.6.
3. *Rajasthan District Gazetteers,* Jaisalmer, op. cit., p.1.
4. Anil Agrawal and Sunita Narayan, eds., *Dying Wisdom, Rise, Fall and Potential of India's Traditional Water Harvesting System,* reprint, CSE, Delhi, 2005, p.107.

5. Ibid.
6. The status of Bikaner does not appear to have been that of an administrative unit but of a convenient grouping of the two well-known states of Bikaner and Jaisalmer. Cf. Irfan Habib, *An Atlas of Mughal Empire*, Oxford University Press, Delhi, 1982, Sheet 6A Rajasthan Political-Notes. He has plotted all the *parganas* of the *sarkar*. There were eleven revenue units (*mahals*) in the *sarkar*, namely Bikampur, Birsilpur, Barmer, Pugal, Pokran, Parker, Jaisalmer, Chohtan, Kotra, Derawar and Bikaner (As quoted by B. L. Bhadani, 'Jaisalmer Settlement Pattern, Dam Technology and Economy in the First Half of the Seventeenth Century', Felicitation Volume of Prof. Agam Kumar Mathur, Dadaji Maharaj Abhinandan Granth, Vol. III, Hajuri Bhavan, Agra, July 27, 1995).
7. *Dastur-ul-amal shahjahani*, British Museum, Add. 6598, ff. 30 a-b, Rotograph in the Department of History, Aligarh Muslim University, Aligarh (As quoted by B. L. Bhadani, 'Jaisalmer Settlement Pattern, Dam Technology and Economy in the First Half of the Seventeenth Century', Felicitation Volume-Prof Agam Kumar Mathur, Dadaji Maharaj Abhinandan Granth, Vol. III, Hajuri Bhavan, Agra, July 27, 1995;
8. *Rajasthan District Gazetteers*, Jaisalmer, op. cit., p.347.
9. Ibid.
10. Ibid.
11. Anil Agrawal and Sunita Narayan, eds., *Dying Wisdom, Rise, Fall and Potential of India's Traditional Water Harvesting System*, op. cit., pp.107-08.
12. Ibid. [According to the editor of the *Protected Monuments of Rajasthan*, this fort is situated on Trikut hill and was founded in AD 1156]. For details see Chandramani Singh, ed., *Protected Monuments of Rajasthan*, Jawahar Kala Kendra, First Edition, Jaipur, 2002, p.239.
13. Ibid. p. 108. [According to information, water from Dabla village, 12 kms from Jaisalmer was taken to the fort from where it was supplied to the whole town. See Anil Agrawal and Sunita

Narayan, eds., *Dying Wisdom, Rise, Fall and Potential of India's Traditional Water Harvesting System*, op. cit., p.108; Vinod Kumar Singh surveyed the area of Jaisalmer, particularly Jaisalmer fort, and he also elaborated its touristic significance. According to him Jaisalmer fort is popularly known as *sonarika* – a golden fort made of yellow sandstone. He has covered the waterworks existing in the enclosed area of the fort and given details of at least seven water-bodies: Jaisal well, Hazaria well, Ranisar well, Vyas well, Jain well, Hauz well and wells at Surajpole. For more details see Vinod Kumar Singh, 'Water Preserving Techniques in Water Scare Rajasthan: An Archaeological Survey of Waterworks in Jaisalmer Fort', in *Ateet: A Journal of History and Archaeology*, ed., M.K. Pundhir, No.1/Vol. 1/July-December-2012, School of Historical Studies , Aligarh, pp.10-19.

14. *Rajasthan District Gazetteers,* Jaisalmer, op. cit., pp.347-48.
15. Ibid.
16. Ibid. [Chandramani Singh explained in details about the temples of Jaisalmer. For details see Chandramani Singh, ed., *Protected Monuments of Rajasthan*, op. cit., p. 240-41.]
17. Anil Agrawal and Sunita Narayan, eds., *Dying Wisdom, Rise, Fall and Potential of India's Traditional Water Harvesting System*, op. cit., p.108. For details regarding Ghadisar tank and other monuments associated with it, see Ranbeer Singh, *Jaisalmer-Vashtushilp, Talab Aur Paryatan,* Shubhi Publications, Gurgaon, 2009, pp.45-78.
18. *Rajasthan District Gazetteers,* Jaisalamer, op. cit., p.346. [Maharawal's favourite dancing girl Tilo built a gateway, a magnificent structure providing entrance on its bank to the lake for the people of the town. The entrance gate of Tilo is named after her. For details see Chandramani Singh, ed., *Protected Monuments of Rajasthan*, op. cit., p.240- 41.]
19. Anil Agrawal and Sunita Narayan, eds., *Dying Wisdom, Rise, Fall and Potential of India's Traditional Water Harvesting System*, op. cit., p.108. [According to Nand Kishore Sharma, it was the only source of water for the people of the town. Rain-water was very carefully collected in this tank. He has also explained that the

water from 15 to 20 kms from the mountains slope particularly from the Bhoo-Bhopa, Jiyaee, thaooba, etc., flowed towards this water tank during the rainy season. See Nand Kishore Sharma, *Jaisalmer Ka Samajik Avam Sanskritic Itihas*, Simant Publication, Jaisalmer, 1993, pp.223-224].

20. B. L. Bhadani, 'Jaisalmer Settlement Pattern, Dam Technology and Economy in the First Half of the Seventeenth Century', op. cit. Cf. *Bankidas-ri-khyat*, ed., Narottam Das Swami, Jaipur 1956, p.203; in the west, too, there are 150 mts high hills. Nainsi records pastures in those area which confirm depression (*khyat*, II, p.8).

21. Ibid., pp. 11-12 and 140.This block contains eighteen villages, but is said to have contained 140 villages earlier.

22. Ibid., p.4.

23. In other areas of the desert *unav* technique was used for irrigation, i.e., Mahajan in Bikaner. See Anupam Mishra, *Aaj Bhi Khare Hain Talaab* and *Rajasthan Ki Rajat Boondein* [*Unav*, it is a low land area where water is collected in the rainy season, and wheat is sown soon there-after]. B. L. Bhadani, ed., *Administration of Bikaner State in the 17th Century*, Sadul Rajasthani Research Institute, Bikaner, 1979, p.83.

24. This *khadeen* system has great similarity with the irrigation methods of the people of Ur (present Iraq) around 4500 B.C. and later the Nabateans in the Middle-East. A similar system is also reported to have been practices 4000 years ago in the Negev desert, and in southwestern Colorado 500 years ago.

25. *Rajasthan District Gazetteers*, Jaisalmer, op. cit., p.1.

26. Ibid.

27. Ibid. [Salim Singh , a Diwan of the state during the reign of Maharaja Moolraj, had levied exorbitant land taxes and collected them from the Paliwals using the strong arm of the state. The Paliwals were the only farming community and owner of almost all the fertile *khadeens* in Jaisalmer. Due to heavy taxation over the Paliwals, they finally decided to leave the place. It is a fact that this was the second large departure and migration of the Paliwals. In fact, these Brahmins were the original residents of Pali, which

was obtained as a land grant from the Parihar Kings of Mandor. Later, Seoji Rathod of Kannauj got many of the Paliwal Brahmins and their chiefs eliminated in an ambush and in AD 1156 gained absolute control of the entire Mandor-Jodhpur region. As these Brahmins have their ancestral home in Pali, they were known as Paliwals. See Ranbir Singh, *Jaisalmer: Art, Architecture & Tourism*, Shubhi Publication, Gurgaon, 2010, pp. 97-101]

28. B.L. Bhadani, 'Jaisalmer Settlement Pattern, Dam Technology and Economy in the First Half of the Seventeenth Century', op. cit.; S.Ali Nadeem Rezavi, 'Kuldhara in Jaisalmer State- Social and Economic Implications of the Remains of a Medieval Settlement', Proceedings of the *Indian History Congress*, 56th Session, Rabindra Bharti, Calcutta, 1995, pp. 312-38; Mayank Kumar, 'Adaption to Climatic Variability: Irrigation and Settlement Patterns in Early Medieval Rajasthan', in *Medieval History Journal*, Sage Publication, Delhi, 2014, pp.57-86.
29. Conducted interviews and survey of the site.
30. *Rajasthan District Gazetteers*, Jaisalmer, op. cit., p.6.
31. Ibid. [The water of the river or rains could be dammed to form a *khadeen*, as was done near Khaba and Masur (the largest *khadeen*-surveyed by Jibraeil (author of this book) and Mr. Zameer Ahmad (Draftman) alongwith Professor B.L. Bahadani). *Khadeen* means an artificial depression created through human labour (effort of farmers, in this case particularly Brahmins), dammed on three sides to collect water. This water, as it evaporates creates soil helpful for agriculture. It seems that most of the *khadeens* were made by the Paliwal Brahmins. After the rains stopped and the water dried up the cereals, like millet (*jowar*), wheat (*gehoon*) and gram (*chana*) would be grown. See S. Ali Nadeem Rezavi, 'Kuldhara in Jaisalmer State - Social and Economic Implications of the Remains of a Medieval Settlement', op. cit., p. 322. Cf. K. D. Erskine, *Rajputana Gazetteers*, The WRS Residency and Bikaner Agency, Allahabad, Vol. III-A, 1901 and III-B,1908, p.25; James Tod, *Annals and Antiquities of Rajasthan*, Vol.II, 1920, p. 1248; and *Rajasthan District Gazetteers*, Jaisalamer, op. cit., p.86.
32. Ibid.

33. Ibid.

34. K.D.Erskine, *The Western Rajputana States Residency and the Bikaner Agency Gazetteer*, 1909, p.5 [According to one record, 95 percent water was not suitable for human consumption. It was being used for animals and some time for irrigation purposes. For details see Hari Ballabh Maheshwari Jaisol, *Jaisalmer Ka Itihas*, The Heritage Publication, Second Edition, Gwalior, 1999, p. 168.

35. *Johad* [A *johad* is a Hindi term frequently used in Rajasthan. It is a rain-water storage tank principally used in the states of Rajasthan and other neighbouring states. Rain-water is collected and stored in it, and used for drinking by humans as well as animals through the year round.].

36. *Rajasthan District Gazetteers*, Jaisalmer, op. cit., p.7.

37. Hari Ballabh Maheshwari Jaisol, *Jaisalmer Ka Itihas*, The Heritage Publication, Second Edition, Gwalior, 1999, p. 168. [There is a noticeable example of a *bundha* (bridge), which is not as small as it usually is, but a big bridge called *Bada bagh* and functions like a *khadeen* for irrigation. It is also called Jaitbandh, and is constructed between two mountains. It was a *bundha* used for the purpose of storing rain-water with the use of *bundh*, a kind of *khadeen*. Near this *Bada bagh*, there are numbers of *pugbao*, constructed to take water easily from these *pugbao*. It was constructed during the reign of Maharawal Jaitsingh in VS 1585/ AD 1528, situated on the Ramgarh road, around 5-6 kms away from the city. The first part of this *bundha* is called Jaitsar, while the other side is known as *Bada bagh*. According to a source, Jaitbandha is around 1200 fts long, 300 fts broad, and its depth (height) is about 100-150 fts. There are five underground canals constructed in the middle of the *bundha*, from these canals water flows in a zig-zag manner from one side to another, locally called *bhawanriya*. The water from here goes to *Bada bagh* via Ramnal, then to *Chhota bagh* and finally reaches to Kshetrapal temple. An excellent device to use the overflowing water is called *nirata*. This extra water generally flows towards saltish Rinn of Ramgarh. Water of this *bundha* was utilized by *Bada* and *Chhota bagh* for

the production of mango, graves, eugenia jambolana (*jamun*), pomegranate (*anaar*), etc. Nand Kishor Sharma, *Jaisalmer Ka Samajik Avam Sanskritik Itihas*, Simant Prakashan, First Edition, Jaisalmer, 1993, pp.233-237].

38. Hari Ballabh Maheshwari Jaisol, *Jaisalmer Ka Itihas*, op. cit., p.167.

39. It is not an easy task to plot every village with its features on the map. Its reliability can only be possible by an exhaustive physical survey, while we have surveyed only a few villages of Jaisalmer. We will take this up in any other work particularly on Jaisalmer State. It is a fact that this area needs more research and survey to understand the techniques use her for irrigation.

40. *Khyat*, p.4. Conducted interviews and survey of the site. Our team measured the largest *khadeen-Masoori* of Jaisalmer in our long survey of the sites.

41. Anil Agrawal and Sunita Narayan, eds., *Dying Wisdom, Rise, Fall and Potential of India's Traditional Water Harvesting System*, op. cit., p.135.

42. Ibid. Also see *Rajasthan District Gazetteers*, Jaisalmer, op. cit., pp.87.

43. Ibid.

44. K.D. Erskine, *Rajputana Gazetteers*, The W.R.S., Residency and Bikaner Agency, Vol. III-A (Allahabad, 1908), p.24.

45. *Khyat*, II, p.5.

46. Ibid., Nainsi gives approximate measurement in terms of 10-15 *baans* (bamboo) which comes around 10 fts in one bamboo.

47. Ibid., One *kos* is equivalent to about 2 ½ miles.

48. *Beri* is generally described as a shallow well. Cf. Sitaram Lalas, ed., *Rajasthan Sabad Kosh*, Vol.III, Chaupasani Shiksha Samiti, Jodhpur, 1972, p.3184; Badri Prasad Sakariya, *Rajasthan Hindi Sabad Kosh,*Vol. II, 1982 ,Jaipur. p.920. The style in which Nainsi records *beri* we may equate it with a channel. However, if it was like a shallow well, then irrigation could have only been possible through some water-lift mechanism. We have explored exact working of *beri* through our physical survey of the sites.

49. *Khyat*, II, p.5.

50. Ibid., It appears that the Persian wheel was used for lifting water from the *Kosita*-well.

51. This point is highlighted by R.C. Sharma, *Settlement Geography of the Indian Desert*, Kumar Brothers, New Delhi, 1972., p.22.

52. *Khyat*, II, p.5.

53. Ibid., p.4. In fact three terms, namely *bujero, khadeen* and *unav* are recorded in one village Thaiat which means existence of three different kinds of depressions.

54. Ibid., Erskine, too, notices (at the turn of this century) these *khadeens* which were constructed by the Paliwal Brahmins, K.D. Erskine, *Rajputana Gazetteers*, op.cit., p.25.

55. Ibid., Erskine notes that a large number of *khadeen* were constructed by the Paliwal Brahmins, but a decline in the number of *khadeen* set in when these people were driven out of the state. [In the absence of perennial streams, and wells too deep to be economically utilized for irrigation purposes, 'artificial irrigation', on any significant scale, is impracticable. The agricultural yield, therefore, has to depend entirely on seasonal rains, which are not only insufficient but undependable too. In parts of the district, particularly around Jaisalmer town where the soil is harder and the surroundings hilly, rain-water from the catchment area flows in small *nallaho (nallah)*, constructed into sort of contour bunds. Minor irrigation is possible from these low -lying accumulations of water, locally termed as *khadeen*. In a few cases, the water thus stored is flown by channels to the adjacent land. But the usual custom is to sow wheat and other grains in the beds of these tanks, manured by the frequently migrating cattle. It is also very interesting to note that due to the absence of any perennial river, a small stream called 'Kakni', flows for a few kms and then turns into 'Bhuj Lake'. Further its water is accumulated in'Daiya Dam'. The river does not irrigate any area, but the wells on its banks get some water through percolation, *Rajasthan District Gazetteers,* Jaisalmer, op. cit., pp.86-87].

56. The survey in the beginning of this century shows existence of 500 *khadeen*. It strengthens our hypothesis of higher number of *khadeen* in the earlier period.
57. We do not have much evidence about the investment in these *khadeen* in the premodern period.
58. Ibid.
59. Ibid., p.27.
60. Ibid.
61. Ibid., pp. 37-88. [A poem composed in praise of Rawal Saliwahan says that he got constructed bridges and tanks. At least it hints at a tradition of rain-water preservation. Our survey work would help to study the tradition of tanks and dams constructed in Rajasthan during the premodern period. Such surveys are also being conducted by our team in other areas of Rajasthan. Many scholars have also worked on it earlier. See Iqtidar Alam Khan and Ravindra Kumar, 'The Mansagar Dam of Amber', in *Technology in Ancient and Medieval India*, eds., A. Roy and S.K. Bagchi, Delhi,1986, pp.25-35; Rajiv Sharma and S. Ali Nadeem Rezavi, 'Aspects of Hydraulic Engineering in Medieval Rajasthan: A Case Study of Water-System in Jaigarh Fort', in *Art and Culture*, eds., A.J. Qaisar and S.P. Verma , Jaipur, 1993, pp.129-32.
62. *Khyat*, II, p.8.
63. Ibid., Erskine mentions about the existence of abundant pasturage in good rainy season. Mention is also made regarding the Pali jungle and other pasturages, and production of good quality of grass, K.D. Erskine, *Rajputana Gazetteers*, op. cit., p. 24.
64. *Rajasthan District Gazetteers,* Jaisalmer, op. cit., pp.98-100.
65. *Khyat*, II, pp.8-9.
66. A poem composed in praise of Rawal Saliwahan, the son of Jaisal, founder of Jaisalmer, transmits information about cattle wealth ('Kavit Bhati Saliwahan - ro)', in *Khyat*, pp.37-38.
67. Cf. Irfan Habib, *An Atlas of the Mughal Empire,* Oxford University Press, Delhi, 1982 (Sheet No. 6B).

68. Ibid. (In the *Bara-Bagh* region, rice (very rare) produced only during the rainy season. This information has been collected during an interview with the knowledgeable persons. This kind of information needs more investigation)

69. Ibid., p.114.

70. Ibid., [Two different qualities of wheat are recorded and their production comes to about 2,00,000 mounds and 3,00,000 mounds, which totals up to 5 lakh maunds of wheat].

71. Cotton was noticed by James Tod in his period. Cf. *Annals and Antiquities of Rajasthan,* op. cit. But not found in the time of Erskine in 1908, K.D. Erskine, *Rajputana Gazetteers*, op. cit., p.23.

72. Census 1921. This table has been prepared by Prof. B.L.Bhadani, which has already been published. He has provided the author a cyclostyle copy of this research paper and suggested him to incorporate this table in the Chapter on Jaisalmer.

■■■

Conclusion

For several centuries surface water-bodies of ancient, medieval and modern period have been serving the people of the desert region, and also the livestock population and wild life. Environmentalists and scholars working on water-bodies are of the opinion that they symbolize an excellent accomplishment of architectural and engineering design. At the same time they symbolize a high degree of community sharing, and economical, social, moral and religious values cast around a desire to obtain water for all living beings in the community. We know that water has always been essential for all living beings in their daily life; therefore, human beings aspire to obtain it by the hardest possible efforts. It is a universally accepted truth that life originated from water, and the existence of all living beings is fully dependent on the availability of water. Human beings have realized the necessity of water in there lives. Particularly in the desert regions like that of Rajasthan, they have tried to develop all possible kinds of well-knit methods to harvest and conserve different types of water, namely underground, surface and rain-water. Through present work, I have convincely and safely tried to conclude that the people in the desert region of Rajasthan successfully created new techniques of water-harvesting and irrigation in areas where there was acute dearth of water.

In our study of the *Water Management System in the Desert Region of Rajasthan (Thirteenth-Eighteenth Centuries)*, we have used a number of archival and non-archival sources, such as *khyat, vigat, sanad parwana bahis, lekha bahis, kamthana bahis; Phalodi-re-jama-kharch-ri-bahi, Nagor-ki ghazal, Bikaner-ki-ghazal, Rajasthan ke pramukh abhilekh, Tawarikh Jaisalmer* and many inscriptions from the Rajasthani, Sanskrit and Persian languages in our first phase of study. In the second phase of our study we started surveying the sites to verify the facts available in the sources, conducted many interviews, and on the basis of above, drafted and concluded six chapters in the present work.

It appears that the people of Marwar (Phalodi and Nagaur) successfully developed the techniques of irrigation and agricultural production in the area, which was known for its dearth of water. The information about the water-bodies was adequately obtained from Nainsi's *Vigat*. Hence, it emerges that the water-harvesting management of all these units was commendable. It is generally believed that the knowledge of the Paliwal Brahmins about the water management was outstanding. They had developed their knowledge both about the surface as well as underground water management, specifically in the desert tracts and built water-bodies accordingly. In true sense they could be called the men of 'Scientific knowledge about water' (Chapter 2 and 3).

In Bikaner, the planners of the wells seem to have knowledge about the science of underground water movement. Since the water-bodies were located on the slope of the tank, therefore, water percolated in the ground would have made an underground passage known in local parlance as *gupt nadi* which passed through the wells and thus raised their water table. It was an exceptional technique of storing rain-water; harvesting every

drop of water after raising the water level of the wells through percolation process (Chapter 4). The existence of a large number of wells in *qasba* Churu shows the availability of subsoil water in abundance in the area. This became possible because of the excavation of tanks in large numbers whose percolated water made it possible. It is also important to note that in the eighteenth century this *qasba* was known as a trade centre. Traders were frequently visiting and staying due to at least one of the reasons, the adequate availability of water (Chapter 5).

Study of water-bodies in Jaisalmer has been a successful attempt to interpretate the data available in Nainsi and to verify it with the survey of the town. In this endeavour, the efforts of peasants to evolve an indigenous dam technology (*khadeen*) are highlighted particularly in premodern times. This technique remarkably suited the desert conditions. It enabled them to grow the maximum number of crops, though some of them needed more water, such as sugarcane, wheat, and even rice too. Maintenance of large pasturages means prosperity in terms of animals and their products which substantially supplemented the peasant's incomes. In the survey of the sites we realized that the people of the town and even rural areas were able to manage the water very efficiently even in the desert land. For instance, they successfully constructed many water-bodies for drinking and possibly for irrigation purposes in the town and village areas. For such purposes they magnificently created a technique called *khadeen* for irrigation in rural and other areas (Chapter 6).

Conclusively I, the author of the book, am safely able to say that the inhabitants of the desert of Rajasthan were successfully able to collect and manage almost every drop of water not only for drinking but for irrigation purposes in many pockets of the region.

■■■

Appendices

Appendix 2.1
Reservoirs in Marwar

S. No.	Name of the *Pargana*	Villages where tanks recorded	Number of tanks	Average per village tanks
1.	Jodhpur	11	36	3.27
2.	Sojhat	157	172	1.09
3.	Jaitaran	75	94	1.25
4.	Siwana	84	96	1.14
5.	Jalor	59	76	1.29
6.	Merta	16	16	1.00
7.	Sanchor	58	69	1.19
8.	Pokaran	34	57	1.68
9.	Phalodi	27	43	1.59
Total		521	659	1.26 Per Vill.

Courtesy to: B.L. Bhadani, *Peasants, Artisans and Entrepreneurs* and Project Report on *'A Physical Survey of Irrigational Works in the Thar Desert of Medieval Times'*

■■■

Appendix 2.2
Urban Water System of Jodhpur (*Pargana* Phalodi)

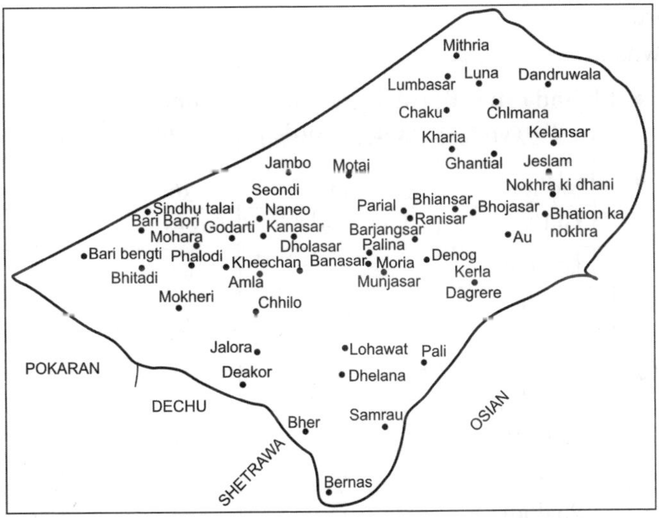

Figure A2.2.1 Settlement pattern of *pargana* phalodi

Courtesy to: B.L. Bhadani, *Peasants, Artisans and Entrepreneurs.*

Appendix 2.3
Phalodi on Trade Routes

According to the sources Phalodi was connected with a number of towns of Rajasthan

- Phalodi to Pugal: *sawa-mandi-sadar-bahi*, no. 11, VS 1822/AD 1765, RSA, Bikaner.
- Jaisalmer to Jaipur: *sanad-parwana-bahi*, no. 13, VS 1830/AD 1773, f.58; and *sanad-parwana-bahi*, no. 20, VS 1835/AD 1778, f.193, Jodhpur records (It is quoted by B.L. Gupta, *Trade and Commerce in Rajasthan During the 18th Century*, Jaipur, 1987, p.131).
- Jaisalmer to Churu: *Jagat-bahi*, no. 81, VS 1807/ AD 1750, Bikaner Records.

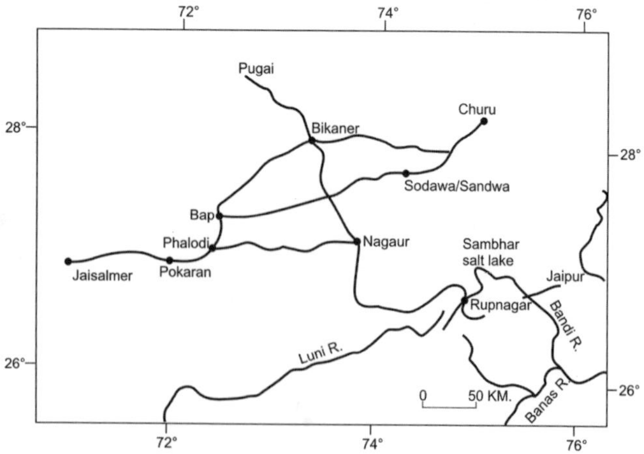

Figure A2.3.1 Phalodi on Trade Routes

Map showing Phalodi, connected with few towns of Rajasthan

1. Phalodi to Pugal : Phalodi-Bap-Bikaner-Pugal
2. Jaisalmer to Jaipur : Jaisalmer-Pokaran-Phalodi-Nagaur-Rupnagar-Jaipur
3. Jaisalmer to Churu : Jaisalmer-Pokaran-Phalodi-Bap-Sodawa-Churu

■■■

Appendix 4.1
Kodamdesar (Bikaner)

Kodamdesar is a small village situated 24 kms west of the city of Bikaner. The Rathor Chief Rao Bika proclaimed himself the overlord near Kodamdesar tank in VS 1529/AD 1472. He planned to have a fort constructed near the tank which was resented to by the local Bhati Chief Rao Sekha. They selected another site where the new city was finally founded in AD 1489. There is a big tank (*talab*) at the former site and on the banks of which is built a temple of Bhairunji.

Figure A4.1.1 A local women taking water for drinking from Kodamdesar talab, Bikaner

According to knowledgeable persons this tank was founded about in 600 years ago. Its catchment area is spread in more than 15 kms, which is well maintained even today because of its religious status. The water-body is surrounded by hilly tracts of *mudiya kankar* which possesses an excellent run off characteristic. The entire catchment's area is made of this material.

The inlet of this tank is very vast and located in its south. According to a local informant, this tank has never been found dry as long as their memory goes. Still villagers use its water for drinking because of its sweetness.

■■■

Appendix 4.2
List of Water Bodies in Bikaner City#

S. No.	Name of the Water-Bodies (Talab/Talai//Baori/Kuwa/others	Year of Construction in VS and AD
1.	Arjun Sagar	VS 1925-50/ AD 1868-1893
2.	Akerajpuri Talai	N.A.*
3.	Bachhesevag Talai	N.A.
4.	Bagariya Talab	N.A.
5.	Bagilai	N.A.
6.	Bakht Sagar	N.A.
7.	Bhaktolai	N.A.
8.	Bhatolai	N.A.
9.	Bhatolai	VS 1920/AD 1863
10.	Binnadi Talai	VS 1781/AD 1724
11.	Bohrolai	N.A.
12.	Brahm Sagar	VS 1953/AD 1896
13.	Chetolai	N.A.
14.	Chhimpolai$	N.A.
15.	Chhogeri Talai	N.A.
16.	Chunagran Talab	N.A.
17.	Darjion Ki Talai	N.A.
18.	Devikund Sagar	N.A.
19.	Dhardidhar	VS 1776/AD 1719
20.	Dhobi Talai	N.A.

21.	Gabolai	N.A.
22.	Garolai	N.A.
23.	Ghadsisar Talab	VS 1944-45/ AD 1887-1888
24.	Girolai	VS 1771/AD 1714
25.	Gogeji Talai	N.A.
26.	Gop Talai	N.A.
27.	Hakolai	N.A.
28.	Hansavat Talai	VS 1887/AD 1830
29.	Harolai	N.A.
30.	Harsolao Talab	VS 1688/AD 1631
31.	Hinglas Talab	VS 1670/AD 1613
32.	Hondolai	N.A.
33.	Jamnolai	N.A.
34.	Jasolai	VS 1882/AD 1825
35.	Jatolai	VS 1961/AD 1904
36.	Kalyan Sagar	VS 1630/AD 1573
37.	Kandolai	VS 1841/AD 1784
38.	Karmisar Talai	N.A.
39.	Kasai Talai	N.A.
40.	Kasiyevali Talai	N.A.
41.	Kharnada	VS 1811/AD 1754
42.	Kisnadi Talai	VS 1832/AD 1775
43.	Kripat Bhairu Talai	N.A.
44.	Kukh Sagar	VS 1937/AD 1880
45.	Lalaniyon Ki Talai	N.A.
46.	Mahanand Talai	VS 1767/AD 1710
47.	Mirjamal Talai	N.A.
48.	Modion Ka Talab	VS 2010/AD 1953
49.	Naee Talai	N.A.
50.	Nath Sagar	N.A.
51.	Naval Puri	VS 1727/AD 1670
52.	Nisani Talai	N.A.

53.	Nrisingh Sagar	VS 1953/AD 1896
54.	Peer Talai	VS 1574/AD 1517
55.	Pharsolai	N.A.
56.	Phoolnath Talab	VS 1777/AD 1720
57.	Radholai	N.A.
58.	Raghunath Sagar	VS 1821/AD 1764
59.	Rajrango Ki Talai	N.A.
60.	Rangolai	N.A.
61.	Sadesevag Talai	N.A.
62.	Sansolao Talab	VS 1572/AD 1515
63.	Savalakhi	N.A.
64.	Shivbari Talab	N.A.
65.	Surajnath	N.A.
66.	Sur Sagar	VS 1614/AD 1557
67.	Thingalbhairu Talai	N.A.
68.	Vishvakarma Sagar	VS 1925/AD 1868
69.	Lakeshwar Baori	N.A.
70.	Juniya Kuwa (old well)	N.A.
71.	Sagariya Kuwa	N.A.
72.	Mohto Ka Kuwa	VS 1956/AD 1899+
73.	Regaron Ka Kuwa++	N.A.
74.	Acharyon Ka Kuwa	VS 1751/AD 1694

#: A Catalogue on '*Water Structures and Monuments of Medieval Northern India*' has been prepared by the author of this book, in association with Prof. B.L. Bhadani in 2011. In this Catalogue, a large number of water bodies of the desert Rajasthan including Bikaner are mentioned.

*N.A. : Not Available (the dates or years of construction is not available)

$: There are two Chhimpolai; one is situated out of the Jasusar Gate and second is out of Hammalo.

+: These may have been inscribed at the time of renovation of the well in the later period.

++: This well was renovated in AD 1940.

Appendix 5.1
Churu: A Centre of Trade and Commerce

Based on *Jagat bahis* (VS 1800/AD 1743, VS 1820/AD 1763) of different years for Bikaner state; *yugpradhan shri jin chandra suri*; M. Elphinstone, *An Account of the Kingdom of Kabul*; Govind Agarwal, *Churu Mandul Ka Shodhpurna Itihas*.

Churu emerged as a prominent trading centre during the 18th-19th centuries because of its location on Delhi-Sindh and Delhi-Kabul routes. It had served as a trade junction. The traders from Northern India used to bring goods to sell here and passed through it to reach other destinations. Some traders also exchanged their goods here with that of the European, Persian, African countries. The traders ordinarily used the following routes which traversed through Churu:

- Bikaner-Agra
- Delhi-Sindh and Delhi-Kabul
- One of the most important routes connected Shakhambari and Ajmer to Sirsa and Bhatinda via Churu, Nohar.
- Godana (Taranagar), a village of Churu was connected with the district Junagarh (Girnar) via Chhapar, Ladanu, and Sanchor, etc.
- Khambhat-Lahore route was the other most important route which passed through Churu.

- An important route leading from Churu connected Rawalpindi, Attuck, Peshawar and Jamrud.
- Mewar-Gaya route too went via Churu.
- One of the routes from Churu was connected with Delhi, Hisar, Ganganagar and Jodhpur.
- Ratangarh-Rajgarh via Churu.

The connecting-link of Churu with major cities of India brought it into prominence in the trading world. The important factor which contributed to the growth of Churu as a large commercial mart in the Northern Rajasthan was that it lay on the route from Multan to Sindh to Jaipur, and Delhi and its internal and external trade connections. This helped to augment the population of this *pargana* headquarter and to develop it into a town with appreciable number of persons. Thus, flourishing trade and commercial activities attracted traders and artisans towards this trading junction which is attested by documents of the pre-census period specifically of the 19th century. The *Jagat bahis* further strengthen the above evidence which indicate the emergence of many *qasbas* in this area because of intense trading activities, namely Churu, Nohar, Reni and Rajgarh, etc.

Appendix 6.1
Water Bodies of Jaisalmer$$

S. No.	Name of the water bodies (talab/talai/ baori/kuwa/others	Year of construction in VS and AD	Remarks
1.	Ghadsisar	VS 1424/ AD 1367	Its early name was Jaisalsar. According to some scholars it was founded by Maharawal Jaisal (the founder of the fort) and its real shape was given by Maharawal Ghadsi.
2	Mool Talab	N.A.**	It was constructed by Maharawal Moolraj. But there is no inscription.
3.	Jagroop Sagar	N.A.	
4.	Bada Bagh/Jaitsar	VS 1585/ AD 1528	It was constructed during the reign of Maharawal Jaitsingh. It is called Jaitbandh. It was a *bandha,* for the purpose of storing of rain-water with the use of *bandh*, a kind of *khadeen*. Near this *Bada bagh*, there are number of *pugbao*, constructed to take water easily from these *pugbao*.

5.	Amar Sagar	VS 1748/ AD 1691	It was constructed by Maharawal Amar Singh and is situated on the way of Lodrava, 40 kms away from the city. Near Amar Sagar many *pugbao* were constructed by the rulers to take water easily. The most important *pugbao* was Anoopbao which was constructed by the immediate queen Anoopde in VS 1749/ AD 1692. It is a kind of *baori* (step-well).
6.	Mool Sagar	VS 1836/ AD 1779	It was constructed by Maharawal Moolrajji II in VS 1836/ AD 1779. Situated on the way of Sam, 8 kms away from the city.
7.	Ganga Sagar	VS 1858/ AD 1801	It was constructed by Maharawal Shri Moolrajji. And is situated on the way of Amarsagar. It is very interesting to know that before the Independence, people who passed through it to go to villages and towards Sindh halted on the banks of this sarovar. This shows its commercial significance. It is quite possible that traders were also staying there on the way to their journey.

8.	Malka Talab	VS 1523/ AD 1466	Constructed by Maheshwari of Mal Nakh, therefore it is called Malka.
9.	Jivanyaee	VS 1561/ AD 1504	It is situated near Mool Talab and Malka Talab and constructed by Khatri Samaj.
10.	Joshisar	N.A.	
11.	Gajroop Sagar	VS 1915/ AD 1858	It was constructed in the name of Maharawal Gaj Singh and his wife Roopkanwar, by Kesari Singhji during the period when his son Ranjeet Singh was ruling. A good technique has been used to collect rain-water in this sagar, and its overflow was channelized towards city with the use of the *nallah*.
12.	Pasvan Asha Ki Talai	N.A.	Near Gajroop Sagar
13.	Darjiyon Ki Chhoti Talai	N.A.	Near Gajroop Sagar
14.	Isarlal Ka Talab	VS 1888/ AD 1831	It was constructed in the memory of Shri Jagannathji by Deewan Acharya Pushkarna Isarlalji. It is situated on the way of Amar Sagar. Its beuty is its *ghat*. Many small well were also constructed in the catchment area (*agor*) of this *talab*.

15.	Hukam Sagar Sarovar	N.A.	Situated just ahead of Isarlal *talab*.
16.	Topa Talai/Nada	VS 1794/ AD 1737	It is also called Kachrey ka topa, because it was constructed by Kachrey Khatri.
17.	Mooley Ki Talai	N.A.	It was constructed by a Muslim Silavat named Mooley. It is situated just ahead of the Jivanyaee, on the way to Gajroop Sagar. The Silavats gathered here every year at the occassion of a fair.
18.	Sudasar Sarovar	VS 1576/ AD 1519	It was constructed by Suda Visani Maheshwari.It is situated on the way leading to Jaisalmer-Barmer road.
19.	Khetasar Sarovar	VS 1607/ AD 1550	It was constructed by Ganga Sut Kheta duing the reign of Maharawal Loonkaran. It is situated near the *dargah* of Sulaiman Peer.
20.	Ratansar Sarovar	N.A.	It was constructed by Ratan Singh, father of Maharawal Ghadsi Rawal. It is situated on the way that leads to Jaisalmer-Pokaran, five kms away from the city.

21.	Vathvaee Talai	VS 1596/ AD 1539	Near Ratansar Sarovar.
22.	Joshisar Sarovar	VS 1856/ AD 1799	It was constructed by Joshi, Chaturbhuj, Hemraj and Premraj. It is situated on Khuhdi road, five kms away from the city, near Tremderai Devi Temple. Nowadays the water of this talab is being used for thousands of animals and few locals as well.
23.	Govindsar	VS 1858/ AD 1801	It was constructed by Laloni Maheshwari during the time of Maharawal Moolraj. It is situated on the road to Barmer.
24.	Govindsar Kuwa	N.A.	It is a very old well and is situated near Govindsar Sarovar.
25.	Gulab Sagar	VS 1952/ AD 1895	It was constructed by Gulabkawar during the period of Maharawal Shalivahan. It is situated just in front of Govindsar.
26.	Dedansar	N.A.	

27.	Chhimpa Talab/ Firojsar	N.A.	It is situated on the way to Jaithwai, 7 kms north of the city, on the bank of the *talab*, *Barahdwari* was also constructed during the Muslim period. Muslim *Chhinpas* were involved in, as washermen and in printing of cloth. Later on they also started working as stone-cutters. According to one source this time there are 100 *Chinpa's* houses in Jaisalmer (around 500 inhabitants: 100 × 5 conventional rate)
28.	Mehtasar	VS 1856/ AD 1799	It is also called as Jaikisansar. It was constructed by Mehta, Ghirat Singh, Salim Singh during the reign of Maharawal Moolraj.
29.	Jaisal well	N.A.	It is circular in shape and is made of yellow-dressed sandstone and mortar. It is situated near Lakshminath temple.
30.	Ranisar Well	N.A.	It is located near the Jaisal well, adjacent to the temple of Lord Shiva and Lakshmi Narayan.

31.	Hazaria Well	N.A.	Irregularly rectangular in shape and located between two temples, i.e., Ratneshwar Mahadev and Lakhmi Narayan temple.
32.	Harjalu Well	N.A.	It is situated in Kundpar.
33.	Boola Well	N.A.	It is situated near the cenotaph of Vyas community. It is also called as villa well.
34.	Vyas Well	N.A.	It is located behind the temples of the Jain community. It is rectangular in its shape.
35.	Ramdesar	N.A.	It is situated below the temple of Ramdevji.
36.	Lakhmansar	N.A.	It is also called Khudiyala, and is situated near Ramdesar well.
37.	Jain Well	N.A.	It is very close to the Jain temple and is rectangular in its shape.
38.	Gusaisar Well	N.A.	It is situated near Isarlalji ki haveli, behind Lakshminathji temple. It is no more in use.
39.	Kotariwala Well	N.A.	
40.	Khariya Well	N.A.	
41.	Wells near Surajpole	N.A.	There are two masonary wells near the Ramdev temple.

42.	Hauz	N.A.	Presently it is under the management of Waterworks Department, though it has been closed by the Rajasthan government.
42.	Mahajansar well	N.A.	It is in the Maheshwari bagichi near Amarsagar.
43.	Chauhansar Well	N.A.	
44.	Gulastala Well	N.A.	
45.	Kesarisar Well	N.A.	It is situated in Chainpura Mohalla, constructed by Kesari Singh.
46.	Sujanpuri ka Kuwa	N.A.	It is situated near Ghadisar pole, Kanya pathshala.
47.	*Beras /Beris* Ghadsisar *Agor*	VS 1931/ AD 1874	Mehta Ajit Singh constructed many *beras* in the catchment (*agor*) area of Ghadsisar talab. This information is available in *Tavariyon ki tarikh.*
48.	Manak Chauk Baori	N.A.	It was constructed in the reign of Gaj Singh. It is situated near Gopa Chauk, behind old Post Office.

49.	Kuldhara Baori	VS 1815/ AD 1758	It was a deep *baori*. A pillar inscription placed near the entrance of the *baori* mentions that Tejmal Kuldhar Brahmin constructed it in VS 1815/AD1758. But at present it is non-functional and filled with sand and rubble.
50.	Kuldhara Wells	N.A.	On the eastern side of Kuldhara settlement, the survey revealed seven wells and a step-well, mentioned above, as Kuldhara baori.

**N.A.: Not Available (the date or year of construction either not available or not found).

$$: The above collected information regarding water structures (*talabs*, wells, *baoris*) is based on the survey by the author of the book, and Mr. Zameer Ahmad (draftsman) with Professor B.L. Bhdani. Author has also been consulted many primary sources and secondary works, and particularly gone through the survey-based works, done by Anupam Mishra, Nand Kishore Sharma, and S. A. Nadeem Rezavi's work on Kuldhara, Mayank Kumar's on *khadeen* and Vinod Kumar Singh's on wells inside the Jaisalmer fort.

■■■

Appendix 6.2
Kuldhara Settlement

Kuldhara, the ruined settlement and site of medieval times, is positioned in the district of Jaisalmer. This abandoned site is plotted on the map as on 26°52′ north latitude and 70°47′ east latitude. According to S. Ali Nadeem Rezavi and verified by our survey team, the whole township revolves around almost centrally located temple which appears to be dedicated to Mother Goddess. The temple is known as the Thakurji's Temple and was the only temple in the *Nagara* style that the village community had erected in the middle of the settlement and installed inside it the idol of Vishnu, as the principal deity in the *sanctum sanctorium*. The township has more than four hundred structures including residential and administrative both. Kuldhara was first settled by a Paliwal named Kadhan, who also dug a tank (*talao*) named Udhansar at Kuldhara. This is mentioned by Lakshmi Chand, the author of *Tawarikh-i-Jaisalmer* and it was also quoted by S. Ali Nadeem Rezavi in his well researched article 'Kuldhara in Jaisalmer State- Social and Economic Implications of the Remains of a Medieval Settlement'. It is noticeable that the water in this seasonal river would raise the groundwater table which could then be tapped by digging wells and step-wells, even after the river had dried up. On the eastern side of Kuldhara the survey revealed seven wells and a step-well (*baori*), most of which are at present non-functional and filled with sand and

rubble. The step-well is located around 125 metres off the main settlement and has its wall height around one metre jutting out from the ground. It is aligned, like the settlement, in a north-south direction (see the ground plan of the Kuldhara *baori*). The protective walls of this old step-well were almost submerged in the sand. About 60 steps go down the shaft of this *baori* that were constructed with the dressed huge slabs of the yellow stone, fitted without any glue. The shaft of the well in the *baori* was sunk at a depth of about 100 fts. It was quite amazing to take note of the fact that the masons had used high engineering skills and techniques to fix heavy stone slabs while constructing a huge edifice such as the *baori*. It was quite possible that as and when it rained, the water from the 'Kak' river must have seeped through the subterrain to trickle into the shaft to fill the well. As long as the people inhabited the village of Kuldhara, the well must had been providing potable water. Therefore, it is said that the step-well as well as some other wells in Kuldhara provided potable water to the community of the settlement and symbolized the continuity of life in this hospitable place.

Figure A6.2.1 Kuldhara Baori

Figure A6.2.2 A Temple View of Kuldhara Settlement

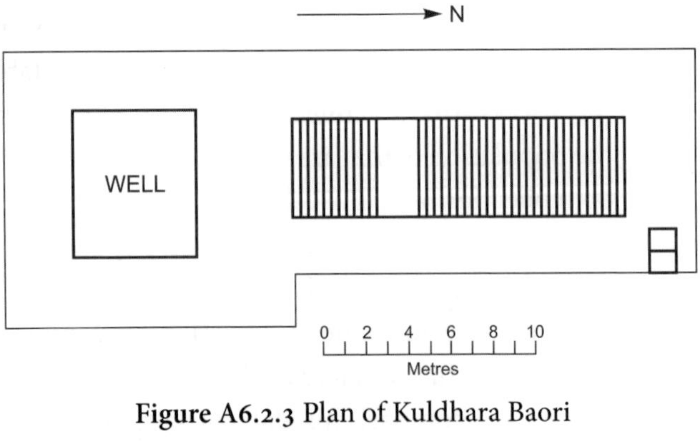

Figure A6.2.3 Plan of Kuldhara Baori

■■■

Appendix 6.3
Jaisalmer's Population

Based on James Tod's, *Annals and Antiquities of Rajashtan*, Vol. I, II, and III also his *Travells of Western India*, (Chapter related to Jaisalmer) and B.L.Cole's, *Census of India, 1931*, Rajputana Agency, Report and Tables, Vol. XXVII, reprint, 1992 (Chapter of towns classified by population).

It is very interesting to note that Col. James Tod had fascination towards population. He made attempts to work out the population of the area about which he was writing. In his pursuit, he always tried to collect data which would help in calculating the population of that area. He had found out number of houses, tax collection and miscellaneous information. This shows his deep interest in the estimation of population. The data collected on town population is extremely useful because it belongs to pre-census period. The information on demography provided by Tod in the first quarter of the 19th century is quite interesting. When we compare his data of Jaisalmer with the Census of 1891, we get more or less the same phenomenon whatever was explained by Professor B.L. Bhadani, mentioned in the table of chapter 6. The details are mentioned below.

The estimation of the population of the towns of Jaisalmer is based on the number of houses and inhabitants collected in 1815 by Tod, which is set out in the following table:

Table A6.3.1 Towns of Jaisalmer (AD1815)

S.No.	Towns	Number of houses	Number of inhabitants
1.	Jaisalmer	7,000	35,000*
2.	Bikampur	500	2000
3.	Sirara	300	1200
4.	Nachna	400	1600
5.	Katori	300	1200
6.	Kaba	300	1200
7.	Kuldharo	200	800
8.	Satla	300	1200
9.	Jinjiniali	300	1200
10.	Devi-Kot	200	800
11.	Bhap	200	800
12.	Balana	150	600
13.	Saliasa	100	400
14.	Baru	200	800
15.	Chaun	200	800
16.	Loharki	150	600
17.	Naontala	150	600
18.	Lahti	300	1200
19.	Dangari	150	600
20.	Bijorai	200	800
21.	Mandai	200	800
22.	Ramgarh	200	800
23.	Birsalpur	200	800
24.	Girajsar	180	600
Grand total		12,350	56,400

*The assumed conventional figure 5 persons per house for Jaisalmer, while for the rest of the towns is 4.

From the above table A6.3.1, it becomes clear that the

towns located in the desert of Jaisalmer area are twenty-four in number and their total number of houses comes to 12350. Further he gives population of each town whose total comes to 56400. For estimation of their population, he applies different ratio for Jaisalmer and other towns. For the former, he obtains population by multiplying the number of houses by 5, while the ratio of 1:4 is applied for the rest. The higher ratio was applied to Jaisalmer because of its status as a capital headquarters. Holding this position, it contains the highest population of 35000, while the lowest inhabitants 400 belong to Saliasa town.

The comparison of population obtained by James Tod for various towns and the corresponding towns' in 1891 would be interesting. This would show the change in the population during the period of eighty years [see Graph A6.3.1].

We have prepared another table A6.3.2 stating the population in 1815 and the population of the same towns in 1891. The Census of 1891 does not provide data for twenty-four towns, but only for Jaisalmer. The probable reason is that the Census of 1891 records the population of only those towns which contained 5000 or more inhabitants. While Tod had mentioned the population of all those places which were called *qasbas* [(see Graph A6.3.2].

Table A6.3.2 A Comparison of Population of Towns of Jaisalmer: 1815 with 1891

S. No.	Towns	Inhabitants in 1815	Inhabitants in 1891
1.	Jaisalmer	35,000	10,509
2.	Bikampur	2000	NA
3.	Sirara	1200	NA
4.	Nachna	1600	NA
5.	Katori	1200	NA
6.	Kaba	1200	NA
7.	Kuldharo	800	NA

8.	Satla	1200	NA
9.	Jinjiniali	1200	NA
10.	Devi-Kot	800	NA
11.	Bhap	800	NA
12.	Balana	600	NA
13.	Saliasa	400	NA
14.	Baru	800	NA
15.	Chaun	800	NA
16.	Loharki	600	NA
17.	Naontala	600	NA
18.	Lahti	1200	NA
19.	Dangari	600	NA
20.	Bijorai	800	NA
21.	Mandai	800	NA
22.	Ramgarh	800	NA
23.	Birsalpur	800	NA
24.	Girajsar	600	NA
Grand total		56,400	10,509

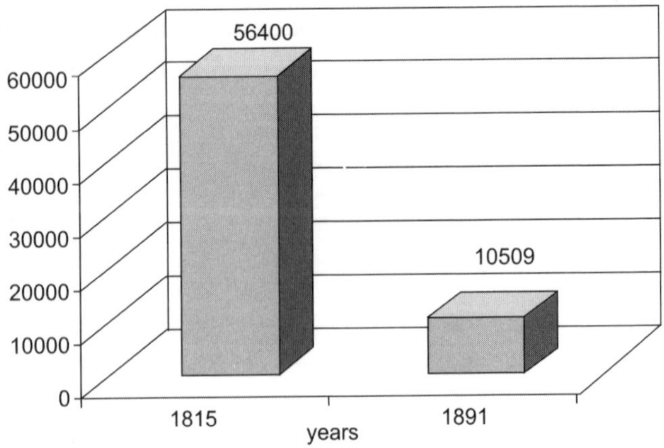

Graph A6.3.1 A comparison of population of the towns of Jaisalmer (1815 with 1891)

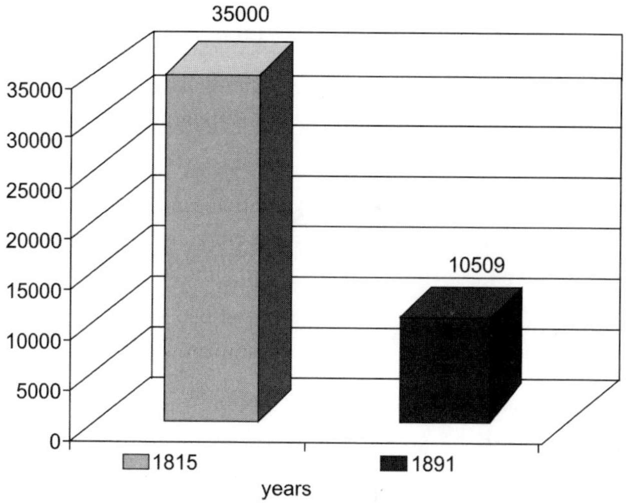

Figure A6.3.2 A comparison of population of Jaisalmer (town only) (1815 with 1891)

Two things emerge from the above comparison: first, all the *qasbas* lost their status in next eighty years; and second, the trend of decline in urban population is visible in the case of Jaisalmer (35000 to 10509)(see Graph A6.3.2). The decline was more than three times which is a clear case of de-urbanization. The effect of the British imports could be seen even in the deep desert of Jaisalmer.

■■■

Glossary

Aab	:	Water.
Aab-i-Zamzam	:	Fresh Water-Body (sacred water).
Abi	:	Irrigation from Tank (*talab*).
Agor	:	Catchments of Tank (*talab*).
Ahar	:	It resembles a rectangular catchment basin with embankments on three sides. Unlike tanks, the beds of *ahars* are not dug out.
Aharyodaka	:	A sort of storage tank with water collected into it through channels.
Akhara Kuwa	:	Deep well. This kind of well is situated away from the rivers in Mewar region.
Araghatta	:	Water-wheels.
Bandha	:	A four-sided tank excavated below *akata* (canal) from which it received water through percolation.
Bandhara	:	A dam in Maharashtra.
Baoli	:	A step-well in India is known as *baoli.*
Baori/Bawari	:	A step-well in Rajasthan is also known as *bavadi* (community well)
Bavdi	:	It is an elaborately and richly ornamented well in Gujarat.

Belagola : A tank with pure water.

Bera : Well (big and large in size).

Beri : Shallow well. Well in the *talab* (lake) bed.

Bhida : Domed-shaped cover of a *kund* (a pit to collect rain-water).

Bier : A wave of water which spreads across the land like a huge sheet, 30-45 cm. deep; this type of flood never cuts the earth.

Boree : Small natural pond.

Bandha : The *bandhs* are made at a levels higher than the fields to be irrigated. These *bandhs* thus prevents the mansoon rain draining away rapidly and are able to supply water to the crops in low-lying the land through slow percolation.

Bugar : A lever to lift water.

Bund : Dam; embankment.

Bundhan : Embankment.

Chahal : A shallow channel.

Chahi : Land irrigated by wells.

Chappris : Small shallow ponds with hardly any masonry work.

Charas : Leather-bucket, Persian wheel.

Cheruvu : Irrigation tank in south India is called *cheruvu*. It is a huge earthen dam built across a stream .

Chuhi : In Punjab state, a small well or reservoir is called *chuhi*.

Dakeriyan	:	Shallow well dug in a harvested field where rain water is impounded for the cultivation, i.e. *kharif.*
Dauri	:	A round shallow basket made of wicker or bamboo matting, used for lifting water.
Deir	:	Water collected in a depression during the rains which dries up by the month of October.
Dhab	:	A water-body in the Thar Desert.
Dhar bund	:	Embankment across hill stream.
Dhenkli	:	A basket with two ropes on each end, used for lifting water.
Dhoras	:	Earthen embankment built across the general slope which conserves the maximum possible rain water run off within the agricultural field.
Doab	:	The area between two rivers.
Dol	:	Water was raised by a dol.
Duar	:	Water channel
Dungs	:	Small irrigation canals linking thats rice fields and a stream (i.e., West Bengal) This technique is also called as *Jampois.*
Gau Ghat	:	A *ghat* of *talab* specifically made for animals.
Hamam	:	Bathroom.
Jhalara	:	*Jhalaras* were man-made tanks, essentially meant for the community use and for religious rites. Often rectangular in shape, having steps on three or four sides.

Johad/Joda	:	Earthen check dams (i.e. Alwar-Rajasthan). [A *johad* is a Hindi term frequently used in Rajasthan. It is a rain water storage tank principally used in the states of Rajasthan and other neighbouring states. It collects and stores water throughout the year, to be used for the purpose of drinking by humans and cattle]. It is also pronounced as Joda.
Khadal	:	The literal meaning of *khadal* appears to be an unleveled land between small hilly areas.
Khadeen	:	It means an artificial depression created by men, dammed on three sides to collect water for irrigation. A *khadeen* is also called a *dhora*. It is an ingenious construction designed to harvest surface run off water for agriculture. Embankment across lower hill slopes.
Khatri	:	Chambers carved in hard rock for storing water (i.e. Himachal Pradesh).
Kohar	:	Large well.
Kosita	:	Deep well.
Kuhl	:	Headwall across a ravine to divert water from a natural stream for irrigation (i.e. Himachal Pradesh).
Kul	:	Water channels in mountain areas (i.e. Jammu, Himachal Pradesh).
Kund/Kundis	:	Underground water storage (i.e. Rajasthan).
Kuwa	:	Big well.

Kuis	:	Found in western Rajasthan; these are 10-12 m deep pits dug near tanks to collect the seepage. *Kuis* can also be used to harvest rain-water in areas with meagre rainfall. *Naada / bandh* : Stone check dam (i.e. Mewar, Thar Desert).
Nadi	:	It is used for storing water from an adjoining natural catchment during the rainy season, generally found in the areas of Rajasthan.
Nirata	:	A kind of technique to use the overflow of water (Jaisalmer).
Paar	:	Area where water has percolated, accessed by *kuis* (i.e. Rann of Kutch, Gujarat).
Rahat	:	Persian Wheel
Ramtek Model	:	Intricate network of groundwater and surface water-bodies, connected through surface and underground canals (Ramtek, Maharashtra).
Rapat	:	Percolation tank (Rajasthan).
Sarovar	:	Big water tank.
Saza Kuva	:	Open well (Mewar, Rjasthan).
Seja Kuwa	:	Shallow well. This kind of well are situated both sides on the banks of river in Mewar region.
Talab/Talao	:	Big water tank
Tankas	:	*Tankas* (small tank) are underground tanks, found traditionally in Bikaner's houses. They are built in the main house or in the courtyard. They were circular

		holes made in the ground, lined with fine polished lime, in which rain-water was collected. Tankas were often beautifully decorated with tiles, which helped to keep the water cool. The water was used only for drinking. If in any year there was less than normal rainfall and the tankas did not get filled, water from nearby wells and tanks would be obtained to fill the household tankas.
Tobas	:	It is the local name given to a ground depression with a natural catchment area. A hard plot of land with low porosity, consisting of a depression; a natural catchment area was selected for the construction of *tobas*.
Unav	:	Natural depression which was being used for production of grains.
Undal	:	Natural depressions created between two ridges.
Virdas	:	Shallow wells (i.e. Rann of Kutch, Gujarat).

■■■

Bibliography

Archival and Non-Archival Records

1. Muhnot Nainsi, *Marwar-ra-pargana-ri-vigat*, ed., Narain Singh Bhati, Vols. I (1968), II (1969), III (1974), Rajasthan Oriental Research Institute, Jodhpur.
2. Muhnot Nainsi, *Khyat*, ed., Badri Prasad Sakariya, Vols. I (1960), II (1962), III (1964) and IV (1967), Jodhpur.
3. *Marwar under Jaswant Singh- Jodhpur Hakumat-ri-bahi* (1658-78), eds., Satish Chandra, Raghubir Singh and G.D. Sharma, Meerut, 1976.
4. *Phalodi bahi*, VS 1701/AD 1644, MSS., RSA, Bikaner.
5. *Hasal-re-lekha-ri-bahi,* VS 1746/AD 1689, RSA, Bikaner.
6. *Marwar-ri-khyat,* MS. *Anup Sanskrit Library,* Bikaner.
7. *Hasal-ri-pargana-ri-bahi,* VS 1746/AD 1689, RSA,Bikaner.
8. *Gaon-re-hasal-ri-bahi,* VS 1746/AD 1689, RSA, Bikaner.
9. *Phalodi-re-jama-kharch-ri-bahi,* VS 1750-51/ AD 1693-94, RSA, Bikaner.
10. *Bankidas-ri-khyats,* ed., Narottam Das Swami, Rajasthan Puratatvanaveshan mandir, Jaipur, 1956.
11. *Jodhpur Records* (non-Archival), RSA, Bikaner. Under this category of documents village-wise information is compiled, which is useful for studying the village profile in water management. This can also be used to make a comparative study with the *Marwar Gazetteer* of Nainsi.

12. *Travelogue of Raj Singh* AD 1677; Raj Singh travelled from Bilara (Jodhpur) to Jamrud crossing entire desert of north Rajasthan. He offers information on the water structures available on the way.

13. B.L.Bhadani, ed., *Administration of Bikaner State in the 17th Century (Bikaner-re-patte-re-gaon-ri-vigat,* AD 1667), Sadul Rajasthani Research Institute, Bikaner, 1979.

14. *Desh Darpan,* eds., J.K. Jain and Girija Shankar Sharma, Rajasthan State Archives, Bikaner, 1989.

15. N.S. Bhati, ed., *Jaisalmer-ri-khyat,* Jodhpur.

16. Yati Udai Chand, *Bikaner-ki-Ghazal,* VS 1765/AD 1708.

17. Yati Manrup, *Nagor-ki-Ghazal,* VS 1862/AD 1805.

18. Uday Chand Matheran, *Bikaner Ghazal,* VS 1763.

19. Different Years of *Kagad bahis* such as;

Bahi No.	VS /AD
1	1811/1754
2	1820/1763
3	1826/1769
4	1831/1774
5	1838/1781
6	1839/1782
7	1840/1783
8	1849/1792
9	1851/1794

25. *Kagad-ri-lekha-ri-bahis*

Bahi No.	VS/AD
192	1865/1808
194	1870/1813
195	1872/1815

26. *Kamthana bahis*

Bahi No.	VS/AD
203	1727/1670
1	1749/1692
135	1759-61/1702-04
10	1821/1764
11	1823/1766
12	1825/1768
205	1829/1772
19	1855/1798
18	1860/1803
16	1869/1812

27. *Lekha and jama kharach bahis*

Bahi No.	VS/AD
44	1686-87/1629-30
45	1716/1659
55	1745-48/1688-91
233	1811/1754
192	1865/1808
250	1877/1820

28. *Sava bahis* of different years, RSA, Bikaner.

29. *Dastur-ul-amal Shahjahani*, British Museum, Add. 6598, ff. 30 a-b, Rotograph in the Department of History, AMU, Aligarh.

30. *Sava-mandi-sadar-bahi*, No. 11, VS 1822/AD 1765, RSA, Bikaner.

31. *Sanad-parwana-bahi*, No. 13, VS 1830/AD 1773, f.58; and *Sanad-parwana-bahi*, No. 20, VS 1835/AD 1778, f.193, Jodhpur records.

32. *Jagat bahi*, No. 81, VS 1807/AD 1750, Bikaner records.
33. *Maru Bharati Patrika*, February 1953 to July 1986.

Travellers Account

1. James Tod, *Annals and Antiquities of Rajashtan*, Vol. I, II, and III, Humphrey Milford, Oxford University Press, London, 1920.
2. James Tod, *Travels in Western India*, Orient Publishers, Delhi, 1971.

Gazetteers/Report

1. P. W. Powlett *(official political agency*, Alwar, 1874), *Gazetteer of the Bikaner State*, reprint, Government Press, Bikaner, 1932.
2. K.D.Erskine, *The Western Rajputana States Residency and the Bikaner Agency Gazetteer*, 1909.
3. K.D. Erskine, *Rajputana Gazetteers*, The W.R.S., Residency and Bikaner Agency, Vol. III-A., (1901) and III-B (Allahabad 1908).
4. *Rajasthan District Gazetteers*, Bikaner, ed., K.K. Sehgal, Government of Rajasthan, Jaipur, 1972.
5. *Rajasthan District Gazetteers*, Churu, ed., K.K. Sehgal, Government of Rajasthan, Jaipur, 1970.
6. *Rajasthan District Gazetteers*, Jaisalmer, ed., K. K. Sehgal, Government of Rajasthan, Jaipur, 1973.
7. *Rajasthan District Gazetteers*, Jodhpur, ed., B.D. Agrawal, Government of Rajasthan, Jaipur, 1979.
8. Reports of the *Archaeological Survey of India*, Vol. II, VI and XXIII.
9. *The Imperial Gazetteers of India*, Vol. XX, Today & Tomarrow's Printers, New Delhi, 1908.

Secondary Works

1. Anil Agrawal and Sunita Narayan, eds., *Dying Wisdom, Rise, Fall and Potential of India's Traditional Water Harvesting System*, reprint, CSE, Delhi, 2005.
2. Anupam Mishra, *Aaj Bhi Khare Hain Talab*, Gandhi Shanti Pratishthan, Second Edition, New Delhi, 1994.
3. Anupam Mishra, *Rajasthan Ki Rajat Bundein*, Gandhi Shanti Pratishthan, New Delhi, 1995.
4. Archibald Adams, *The Western Rajputana States, A Medico-topographical & General Account of Marwar, Sirohi & Jaisalmer*, London , (first published 1899), 1990.
5. Archibald Adam, *The Western Rajputana State*, Second Edition, London, 1900.
6. B.L. Bhadani, *Peasants, Artisans and Entrepreneurs, Economy of Marwar in the Seventeenth Century*, Rawat Publication, Jaipur, 1999.
7. B.L.Bhadani, *Water Harvesting, Conservation and Irrigation in Mewar (AD 800-1700)*, Manohar, Delhi, 2012.
8. B.L. Gupta, *Trade and Commerce in Rajasthan During the 18th Century*, Jaipur Publishing House, Jaipur, 1987.
9. B.Ray, *Census 1961: West Bengal District Census Handbook*, Bankura, 1967.
10. Braj Ratan Joshi, *Jal Aur Samaj*, Pustak Sansar, Jaipur, 2005.
11. Chandramani Singh, ed., *Protected Monuments of Rajasthan*, Jawahar Kala Kendra, Jaipur, First Edition, 2002.
12. Chetan Singh, *Punjab in the Seventeenth Century*, Oxford University Press, Delhi, 1988.
13. Dashrath Sharma, ed., *Rajasthan Through the Ages*, Vol. I, Rajasthan State Archives, Bikaner, 1966.

14. G.H. Ojha, *The History of Rajputana*, Vol. 1, Ajmer, 1937.
15. G.H. Ojha, *Bikaner Rajya Ka Itihas*, pt.-I, First Edition, Ajmer, 1939.
16. G.H.R. Tillotson, *The Rajput Palaces 1450-1750*, New Haven and London, 1987.
17. Govind Agarwal, *Churu Mandal Ka Shodhpurna-Itihas,* Lok Sanskriti Sodh Sansthan, Churu, 1974.
18. Govind Lal Srimali, *Rajasthan Ke Abhilekh,* 2 Vols. Maharaja Man Singh Pushtak Prakash, Fort Jodhpur, 2000.
19. G.N. Sharma, *Social Life in Medieval Rajasthan*, (1500-1800), L.N. Agarwal, Agra, 1968.
20. Hari Ballabh Maheshwari Jaisol, *Jaisalmer Ka Itihas*, The Heritage Publication, Second Edition, Gwalior, 1999.
21. H.C.Verma, *Harvesting Water and Rationalization of Agriculture in North Medieval India (Thirteenth–Sixteenth Centuries),* Anamika Publishers, Delhi, 2001.
22. Irfan Habib, *Agrarian System of Mughal India*, second revised edition, Oxford University Press, Delhi, 1999.
23. Jutta Jain Neubauer, *The Step Wells of Gujarat in Art Historical Perspective,* Abhinav Publication, New Delhi, 1981.
24. K.C. Jain, *Ancient Cities and Towns of Rajasthan,* Motilal Banarasidass, Delhi, 1972.
25. Lakhmi Chand, *Tawarikh-Jaisalmer, Chirag Rajasthan Yantralaya,* Ajmer, 1891; rept. 1999, pub. by Rajasthani Granthagar, Jodhpur.
26. Mangilal Vyas 'Mayank', *Rajasthan Ke Abhilekh*, Rajasthan Sahitya Mandir, Jodhpur, 1980.
27. M.H.Siddiqui, *Madhya Kaleen Nagaur Ka Itihas*, Maharaja Mansingh Pustak Prakash, Jodhpur, 2001.
28. Nand Kishore Sharma, *Jaisalmer Ka Samajik Avam Sanskritic Itihas*, Simant Publication, Jaisalmer, 1993.

29. N.K.Sharma, *Golden Town Jaisalmer*, Jaisalmer, 1980.
30. R. A. Agrawal, *History, Art and Architecture of Jaisalmer*, Delhi, 1979.
31. Ranbir Singh, *Jaisalmer-Vashtushilp, Talab Aur Paryatan*, Shubhi Publications, Gurgaon, 2009.
32. Ranbir Singh, *Jaisalmer: Art, Architecture & Tourism*, Shubhi Publication, Gurgaon, 2010.
33. R.C. Sharma, *Settlement Geography of the Indian Desert*, Kumar Brothers, New Delhi, 1972.
34. R.L. Singh, *India: A Regional Geography, National Geographical Society of India*, reprint, Varanasi, 1987.
35. Sureshwara Nand, *Art and Architecture of Jaisalmer*, Jodhpur, 2001.
36. V.C. Mishra, *Geography of Rajasthan*, National Book Trust, New Delhi, 1967.

Research Papers/Articles

1. A.J. Qaisar, 'Agricultural Technology Depicted in Mughal Paintings', in *Itinerario*, Vol. XVI, No.2, Leiden (Grafaria), 1992.
2. A.J. Qaisar, 'Agricultural Technology in Mughal Paintings' in *Medieval India 3 Researches in the History of India* ed., B.L.Bhadani, Manohar, Delhi, 2012.
3. B.D. Chattopadhyaya, 'Irrigation in Early Medieval Rajasthan, *Journal of the Economic and Social History of the Orient*, Vol. XVI, pt. II, III, Leiden, 1973.
4. B.L. Bhadani, 'Indra Sarovar Dam: In Service of the Royal Family Deity and the People', Felicitation Volume of Professor Anand Krishna, *The Anandvana of Indian Art*, 2004.

5. B.L.Bhadani,'Jaisalmer Settlement Pattern, Dam Technology and Economy in the First Half of the Seventeenth Century', Felicitation Volume of Prof. Agam Kumar Mathur, Dadaji Maharaj Abhinandan Granth, Vol. III, Hajuri Bhavan, Agra, July 27, 1995.
6. B.L. Bhadani, 'Udai Sagar: A Sixteenth Century Dam in Udaipur', *Medieval India-2*, ed., Shahabuddin Iraqi, Manohar, Delhi, 2008.
7. B.L. Bhadani, 'Well-irrigation in Marwar in the 17th Century', *Shodh Patrika,* Vol. 40(1), Udaipur, 1990.
8. B.L.Bhadani and Jibraeil, 'Techniques of Irrigation in the Desert area of Phalodi in Medieval Times', *PRHC,* Bikaner, 2008.
9. B.L.Bhadani and Jibraeil 'Water Harvesting and Techniques of Irrigation in Urban Areas During Medieval Period: A Case Study of Bikaner', in seminar proceedings *Urbanization and Trade Routes of Rajasthan*, ed., S.P. Vyas, Book Treasure, Jodhpur, 2011.
10. David Hardiman, 'Well Irrigation in Gujarat: Systems of use Heirarchies of Control' in *Economic and Political Weekly,* Vol. XXXIII, Sameeksha Trust Publication, Mumbai, June-1986.
11. Elizabeth Whitecombe, 'Canal Irrigation and Ecological Change in Colonial North India', Ramchandra Guha, ed., *Social Ecology*, Oxford University Press, Delhi, 1994.
12. Govind Agarwal, 'Rajasthan Ke Jan-Jeevan aur Lok Sahitya main Oont', *Maru Bharti,* Vol. 13(1), 1965–66.
13. Ghan Shyam Lal Devra , 'A Study of the Trade Relations between Rajasthan and Sindh-Multan (1650-1800 A.D.)',

A Chapter in his edited book *Socio-Economic History of Rajasthan*, Shri Jagdish Singh Gahlot Research Institute Jodhpur, 1980.

14. Ghan Shyam Lal Devra, 'Desertification and Problems of Delimitation of the Rajputana Desert during the Medieval Period', in *Rajasthan Ecology, Culture and Society*, eds., M.K. Bhasin and Veena Bhasin, Delhi, 1999 (a).
15. Ghan Shyam Lal Devra, 'Problems in the Delimitation of the Rajputana Desert During the Medieval Period', in *Desert, Drought & Development: Studies in Resource Management and Sustainability*, ed. Rakesh Hooja and Rajendra Joshi, Jaipur, 1999 (b).
16. Hem Sharma, 'Bikaner Ke Talab' in *Rajasthan Patrika* in 1993.
17. Iqtidar Alam Khan and Ravindra Kumar, 'The Mansagar Dam of Amber', in *Technology in Ancient and Medieval India*, eds., Anirudh Ray and S.K. Bagchi, Sandeep, Delhi, 1986.
18. Iqtidar Alam Khan, 'Structure, Location and Working of a Seventeenth Century' paper presented to the *Indian History Congress*, 1984 (cyclostyled).
19. Irfan Habib, 'Technology Changes and Society-13th and 14th Centuries' (Presidential Address), Varanasi, *PIHC*, 1969.
20. Jibraeil, 'Churu: A City of the Desert', in a Journal *Shodh Patrika,* Year 53, Ank 1-4, Institute of Rajasthan Studies, Udaipur, January-December- 2002.
21. Jibraeil, 'Tod's Estimation of Population of Some Urban Centres of Rajasthan: A Case Study of Jaisalmer', in the

Felicitation Volume *Studies in Indian History and Culture,* eds., I.H.Ansari, H.A.Qureshi and al-Taimi al-Siddiqi, Idarah-i Adabiyat-i Delli, New Delhi, 2010.

22. Jibraeil, 'A Study of Water Harvesting Technique and Its Supply at Nagaur Fort', in *Water Resource Management in India: A Historical Study*, ed., S.P. Vyas, Triveni Publication, Jodhpur, 2011.

23. Jibraeil, 'Water Harvesting Techniques of Desert Rajasthan: A Sample Study of *Qasba* Churu, Chhapar and Bidasar', in a Research Journal *Juni Khyat*, Ank 1-2, Maru Bhumi Shodh Sansthan, Shri Dungargarh, Bikaner, 2014.

24. Jibraeil, 'A Technique of Irrigation and Agricultural Production in *Qasba* Nagaur', in a Research Journal *Shodh Sadhana*, Year 29, Ank 25, Natnagar Shodh Sansthan, Sitamau, Madhya Pradesh, 2014.

25. Jibraeil, 'Cultural Significance of Water Harvesting Monuments in *Qasba* Nagaur: Shamsi Talab A Living Evidence', in a Seminar Proceeding *Sources of Cultural History of India*, ed., Manohar Singh Ranavat, Natnagar Shodh Sansthan, Sitamau, Madhya Pradesh, 2013.

26. Jibraeil, 'Structural Remains of Water Management in *Qasba* Nagaur in the Light of Composite Culture', in a book *Composite Culture-A Reappraisal the Cultural Structure of Indian Society* ed., Omprakash Srivastav, Germany, 2012.

27. Jibraeil, 'Socio- Religious and Cultural Monuments in Medieval Rajasthan: A Case Study of Kolayat Sarovar' in the Felicitation Volume *Aspects of Indian History and Culture*, Idarah-i Adabiyat-i Delli, New Delhi, 2011.

28. Jibraeil, 'Cultural Importance of Water Harvesting Monuments in Medieval Rajasthan' in a Research Journal *Shodh Sadhana*, Year 26, Ank 22, Natnagar Shodh Sansthan, Sitamau, Madhya Pradesh. 2011.

29. Jibraeil, '*Qasba* Nagaur : A Centre of Trade and Commerce During Delhi Sultanate', in a seminar proceeding *Re-Interpretating History of the Delhi Sultanate*, ed., Ali Athar, Woodpecker publication and Publication Division, Aligarh Muslim University, First Edition, Aligarh, 2014.

30. L.P. Tessitori, A Progress Report on the work done during the 1916 in connection with the Bardic and Historical Survey of Rajasthn, Journal, *Asiatic Society*, Vol. XIII, 1917, No. 4.

31. Mayank Kumar, 'Adaption to Climatic Variability: Irrigation and Settlement Patterns in Early Medieval Rajasthan', in *Medieval History* Journal, Sage Publication, Delhi, 2014.

32. M. K. Pundhir, 'Banjaron Ki Baori at Sikar (Rajasthan): A Study of Medieval Hydraulic Technology' in *Medieval India 3-Researches in the History of India*, ed., B.L. Bhadani, Manohar, Delhi, 2012.

33. Mohammad Afzal Khan, 'Urban and Palace Water-Works during the Mughal Period', *Puratatva* No. 9, Indian Archaeological Society, Delhi, 1988-89.

34. Neelima Vashishtha, 'A Note on the Sculptures of the Raj Samudra Lake in Rajasthan', in *Art and Architecture* (Felicitation Volume in the Honour of Professor S. Nurul Hasan), eds., A.J. Qaisar and S.P.Verma, Publication Scheme, Jaipur, 1993.

35. Rajendra Kumar, 'Paani Peechh-Ek Jalprabandhan: Bikaner Rajya Ke Vishesh Sandarbh Mein', *PRHC*, Vol. XXVIII, Jaipur, 2012.

36. Rajiv Sharma, 'Raj Samand Dam: An Achievement of the 17th Century Civil Engineering', *PIHC*, 1992-93.

37. Rajiv Sharma and S. Ali Nadeem Rezavi, 'Aspects of Hydraulic Engineering in Medieval Rajasthan: A Case Study of Water-System in Jaigarh Fort', A.J. Qaisar and Som Prakash Verma, eds, *Art and Culture*, Abhinav Publishers, Jaipur, 1993.

38. R. Thomas Rosin, 'Locality and Frontier: Securing Livelihood in the Aravalli zone of Central Rajasthan', *The Idea of Rajasthan*, II, eds., Karine Sahomer, Joan L. Eradman, Desyck O. Lodrick and Lylord I. Rudolf, Delhi, 2001.

39. S. Ali Nadeem Rezavi, 'Kuldhara in Jaisalmer State-Social and Economic Implications of the Remains of a Medieval Settlement', Proceedings of the *Indian History Congress*, 56th Session, Rabindra Bharti, Calcutta, 1995.

40. Vinod Kumar Singh, 'A Chandella Reservoir: Kalyan Sagar of Mahoba', *PIHC*, 53rd Session, Warangal, 1992-93.

41. Vinod Kumar Singh, 'Water Preserving Techniques in Water Scare Rajasthan: An Archaeological Survey of Waterworks in Jaisalmer Fort', *Ateet: A Journal of History and Archaeology*, ed., M.K. Pundhir, School of Historical Studies, Aligarh, 2012.

Atlas/Census

1. *Agricultural Statistics of Marwar*-World Agricultural Census (Type Script), Mehkamakhas, Government of Jodhpur, 1929-30.

2. B.L. Cole, *Census of India*, 1931, Rajputana Agency, Report and Tables, Vol. XXVII, reprint, 1992.

3. *Census Map* of Jodhpur.

4. *Census of India*, Vol. I, Part II-A

5. Irfan Habib, *An Atlas of Mughal Empire*, Oxford University Press, Delhi, 1982.

6. *The Geological Survey of India*, Vol. XXXVIII, 1908.

7. *National Atlas of India*, Jaipur Plate, No. 113, 1951, (Population), 1960.

8. *World Agricultural Census: Statistics of Marwar*, 1929-30 (Typescript), RSA, Bikaner.

Journal

1. *Indian Economic and Social History Review.*
2. *Indian Geographical Journal.*
3. *Indian Historical Review.*
4. *Journal of the Rajasthan Institute of Historical Review.*
5. *Journal of Uttar Pradesh Historical Society.*
6. *Medieval Indian Journal, Sage.*
7. *Juni Khyat.*
8. *Proceedings, Indian History Congress.*
9. *Proceedings, Rajasthan History Congress.*
10. *Social Scientist.*
11. *Shodh Patrika.*
12. *Shodh Sadhana.*

Dictionary

1. Amba Prasad Suman, *Krishak Jeevan Sambandhi Braj Bhasha Shabd Kosh,* Allahabad, 1960.
2. Badri Prasad Sakariya, *Rajasthan Hindi Sabad Kosh,* Vol I (1977), Vol. II (1982), Vol. III (1984), Jaipur.
3. F. Steingass, *Comprehensive Persian- English Dictionary,* Oriental Books, New Delhi, 1981; Lowe and Brydone Printers, London, 1892, 1930.
4. G. Watt, *The Dictionary of the Economic Products of India,* 6 Vols., London, 1889-1993.
5. Sitaram Lalas, ed., *Rajasthan Sabad Kosh*, Chaupasani Shiksha Samiti, Jodhpur, 1972.
6. S.V. Apte, *Sanskrit-English Dictionary*, Motilal Banarasidass, Delhi, 1959.

■■■

Index

A

B

C

D

M

N

■■■